TOMMYWOOD *jr., jr.*

THE *Gospel* ACCORDING TO TOMMYWOOD

From Award-Winning Journalist and Producer

TOM TEICHOLZ

The Fourth Installment of the ***TOMMYWOOD*** Series, a Collection of Columns and Writing on Arts and Culture

A PONDWOOD PRESS BOOK

PONDWOOD PRESS
1424 4th Street, Suite 229
Santa Monica, CA 90401

FIRST TRADE PAPERBACK EDITION

The majority of the articles in this collection first appeared in print in *The Jewish Journal of Los Angeles*, some in slightly different form and can also be found at tommywood.com.

ISBN: 978-0-9883964-7-0

Set in Minion
Printed in the United States

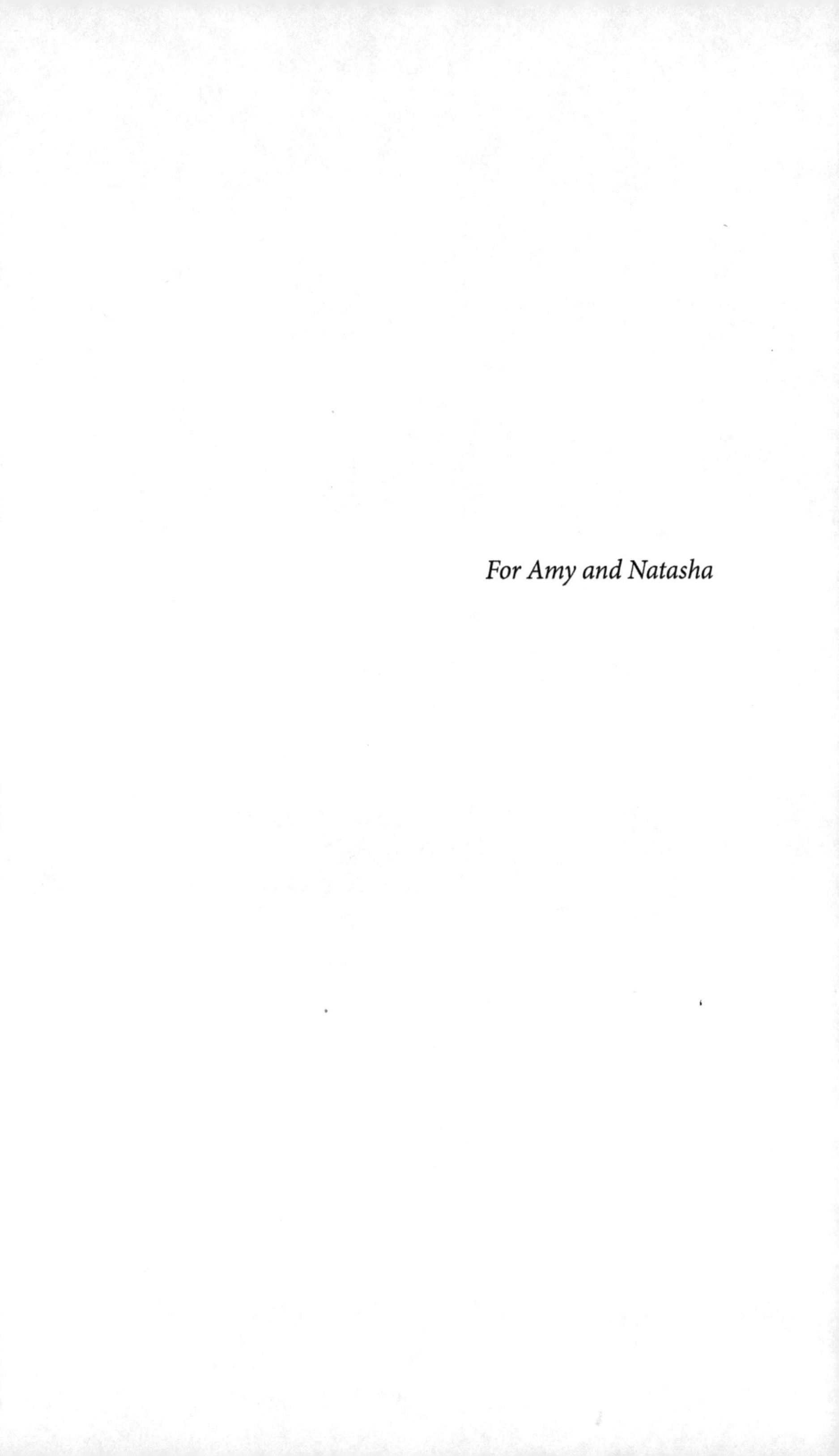

For Amy and Natasha

CONTENTS

INTRODUCTION

In this volume of *Tommywood,* I was fortunate to have the opportunity to share the story of Hatschek Bela, my great-grandfather and the first person in Hungary to own a car; as well as to chew over what is museum worthy; to revisit the sixties; expound about about comic books; to attend an Adam Sandler press conference; to watch every film version of works by Philip Roth. I was able to meet Art Spiegelman and hang out with Herb Gold, and to think long and hard about movies whose subject is the Holocaust.

But there's more: I was in heaven while interviewing Mel Brooks who flattered me by laughing at one of my jokes and who spontaneously started singing to me. I got to renew my acquaintance with Ricky Jay, Robert Kraft, meet Rabbi David Wolpe as well as the women behind Vidiots, and rethink the Kasztner case.

In *Tommywood, Jr., Jr.*, we look to the future: social media makes its first appearance, as I predict Facebook's imminent ubiquity; as well as to the past when a Los Angeles store features the furniture of Hungarian modernist architect and designer

Lajos Kozma; and a documentary establishes a Jewish connection to basketball. Go figure.

Better yet, go read. *Tommywood Jr Jr: The Gospel According to Tommywood* awaits.

TRAWLING FOR BOOKS

BookExpo, the annual convention of booksellers and book publishers that took place in Los Angeles recently, is the book industry's annual get-together, alternating among the publishing hub of New York and various other cities, such as Miami, Chicago, Washington, DC, and Los Angeles.

Perhaps it's the state of the book industry, the economy or just the cost of gas, but this year's convention was not as well attended as in past years. The last time Book Expo was in Los Angeles, the convention floor was constantly, overwhelmingly crowded, with so many booths that the author autographing section had to be relegated to a basement hall.

This time, many editors did not even make the trip, and some publishers or imprints decided not to pay for a stand. For example, I was surprised that Bloomsbury USA didn't have one, given that they represent several Los Angeles authors with just-published or forthcoming books, including Seth Greenland (*Shining City*), Rachel Resnick (*Love Junkie*) and Mark Sarvas (*Harry, Revised*). Still, the smaller turnout really didn't put a damper on the excitement, the conviviality and the parties, which seemed to take over Los Angeles from downtown to West Hollywood, Beverly Hills, Bel Air, and Santa Monica.

At BookExpo, publishers were not only showcasing current titles, they also were trying to create excitement for books that will come out this summer and fall. Translation: Free books were given out.

Among the those I sought while trawling the aisles were the highly anticipated Salman Rushdie novel, *The Enchantress of Florence* (which is already receiving decidedly mixed reviews), Oscar Hijuelos's *Dark Dude (*Atheneum) and Andre Dubus III's *The Garden of Last Days,* which is shaping up to be a novel of major importance.

Among the stacks of desired new books were John LeCarre's *A Most Wanted Man* (Knopf), Dennis Lehane's *The Given Day* (Morrow), Michael Connolly's *The Brass Verdict* (Hachette) and Wally Lamb's *The Hour I First Believed* (HarperCollins). Harper is also pushing Alafair Burke's *Angel's Tip*—if the name seems familiar, it's because Burke's father, James Lee Burke, writes the Dave Robicheaux series.

Just as from small acorns grow large oak trees, small presses sometimes deliver great novels. Steerforth Press, which published Karoly Pap's *Azarel,* an undiscovered gem of a novel of pre-war Hungary, was at the convention with Benjamin Taylor's *The Book of Getting Even,* which Philip Roth has already hailed as: "Among the most original novels I have read in recent years."

This September, Algonquin books will publish Ariel Sabar's *My Father's Paradise: A Son's Search for his Jewish Past in Kurdish Iraq.* Sabar is a political reporter for the Christian Science Monitor covering this year's presidential campaign. His father, Yona Sabar, is a UCLA professor. The book tells of their father-and-son journey to today's postwar Iraq to visit Yona's birthplace and to reconcile past and present.

Speaking of fathers and sons, Adam Nimoy, son of you-can-guess-who, has written *My Incredibly Wonderful, Miserable Life,* which Simon and Schuster has dubbed a "hilarious anti-memoir" about facing life "as a newly divorced father, a fortysomething in the LA dating scene, a recovering user and a former lawyer turned director turned substitute teacher…in search of his true self."

Among the grand dames signing books were Jackie Collins (I passed) and Barbara Walters (I waited in a long line to get a signed copy of *Audition* [Knopf]).

No one likes the expression "chick lit," but what should we call light reads targeted at the *Sex and the City* audience? Female-driven entertainment? Part of the problem is that this grab-bag term encompasses quasi-literary fiction (*Bridget Jones*), commercial fiction (*The Starter Wife*) and a sort of gossipy insider's revenge book (*The Devil Wears Prada*).

Call them what you like, but buy them you will. Some female-friendly titles you may spot this summer or in early fall include former E! hostess Jules Asner's *Whacked* (Weinstein Books), Julie Buxbaum's *The Opposite of Love* (Dial Press), Claire Lazebnik's *The Smart One and The Pretty One* (5 Spot), subtitled: *A Novel about Sisters*—(I happen to know one of the sisters, Nell Scovell, but I'm not saying which one I think she is)—and Jodi Wing's *The Art of Social War* (HarperCollins), which has already been sold to the movies.

Speaking of politics—and who isn't these days?—Public Affairs, a division of Perseus Group, is the publisher of Scott McLellan's book, and it has had no problems getting publicity for the book. It also has a book forthcoming about censorship that should generate some debate called, *Obscene in the Extreme,* an account of the burning and banning of John Steinbeck's *Grapes of Wrath.* It's by Rick Wartzman, a senior Irvine Fellow of the New America Foundation and a former Los Angeles Times Magazine editor.

Public Affairs was launched in 1997 by Peter Osnos, my former editor at Times Books, and I was very happy to run into him, looking dapper as ever, at the Hotel Bel Air, where he was hosting a BookExpo party.

That same night, the New York Review of Books also hosted a party at the Bel Air, and it's worth commending it not only for its party-giving skills, but for its publishing program. Recently, the NYRB Classics have brought back into print editions of Vassily Grossman's masterpiece, *Life and Fate,* and the Yiddish classic, *The Family Mashber* by Der Nister.

Most recently, it published new editions of Stefan Zweig's final novel, *Chess Game,* and his earlier novella, *The Post Office Girl.* Zweig, who committed suicide in 1940, was one of the most-published authors of the first half of the 20th century. The NYRB editions are getting rave reviews and returning Zweig to the popular consciousness.

One of the most interesting and companiable hours I spent at the BookExpo was speaking to Nicolas Neumann, a Paris-based art house publisher. Our meeting occurred because, as I was wandering past his booth, I heard him speaking French. When I looked up to see the name of his booth, Somogyi, I had to stop.

Eva Somogyi was my mother's stage name in Budapest, so I turned to Neumann and asked point blank: Hungarian or French? The answer, not surprisingly, was both—the original founder, Somogyi, was of Hungarian parentage, but the publishing house is French. Somogyi turns out to be one of the largest publishers of museum exhibition catalogs in France.

Upon learning that my column appears in The Jewish Journal of Greater Los Angeles, Neumann immediately directed my attention to two of his English-language books. One of them is *Human Expressionism: The Human Figure and the Jewish Experience,* the companion book to an exhibition this spring at the Musee Tavet-Delacour in Pontoise, a suburb of Paris. The book illustrates a fantastic and very thought-provoking exhibition featuring works by Soutine, Modigliani, Pissaro, Mane-Katz, Lasar Segall, Kitaj and Serge Strosberg, with a wonderful essay by Eliane Strosberg.

Neumann also showed me a book of the death camp drawings of Shelomo Selinger—really remarkable, haunting work that deserves an American exhibition (Skirball people, are you listening?).

Speaking of art, but on a definitely lighter note, I was happy to run into the folks from BukAmerica—Gary Kornblau and Lisa Lyons, whose Hollywood-based publishing house creates $1.49 pamphlets that run the gamut from reprints to original works, from a translation of Baudelaire, to the U.S. Constitution, from Ruth Reichl's *The Queen of Mold* to Richard Grossman's *Glossary of Every Humorous Word in the English Language.* (Example: "agnify: to dress up as a sheep.")

Also from the local scene was Ammo, an LA-based publisher started by Steve Crist, who does very hip books like *Gonzo,* about Hunter Thompson, and a series of books by the designer Todd Oldham, including one about John Waters with an essay by Cindy Sherman.

And if you like local, there's Angel City Press, where Paddy Calisto continues to publish fine volumes on Los Angeles' history and culture. I even met Gidget herself, Kathy Zuckerman, at the Santa Monica Press booth, where she and Dominic Priore were signing posters for *Pop Surf Culture: Music, Design, Film and Fashion from the Bohemian Surf Boom,* available in September.

Children's books occupied a fair amount of real estate at BookExpo. One title that particularly appealed to me was *My Name is Gabito (Me Llamo Gabito)* an English- and Spanish-language children's book about the life of Gabriel Garcia Marquez by Monica Brown, who asked me, "And how many Latina Jews do you know?" (More than you think, mi amiga).

And as long as we are taking a walk on the Semitic side of the street, I was pleased to stumble on Lerner Publishing Group. It recently acquired Kar-Ben Publishing, "a growing Jewish library for children," which includes everything from Yale Strom's first children's book, *The Wedding That Saved a Town,* to biographies, books about Israel, books about Jewish holidays and books about families and friends that encompass many religions.

Meanwhile, over at Matzoh Ball Books (that is their name!), Anne-Marie Baila Asner has just published *Klutzy Boy* (prior titles include *Kvetchy Boy, Schmutzy Girl, Noshy Boy,* and *Schluffy Girl*). Let the imagination run wild.

Now, if having your child learn a foreign language grabs you, Slangman Publishing has a series for ages three and up, where familiar fairy tales, such as *Cinderella,* are retold with foreign words to build up a child's vocabulary in a foreign language (there's an audio CD included, as well). Languages include Chinese, French, Spanish, Hebrew, Italian, and Japanese.

Perhaps this is a good time to talk about "Mo's Nose." My daughter's homework folder has recently been covered with stickers about a dog named Mo. I now know why.

Turns out one of my daughter's classmates is the son of Margaret Hyde, the author of children's books such as *Dreadilocks and the Three Slugs* and the *Great Art for Kids* series (*Picasso for Kids, Matisse for Kids*). Hyde has now launched *Mo's Nose,* a series of books for children about a dog named Mo and how although he doesn't see in color, he can smell colors. The books, illustrated by Amanda Giacomini, have an innovative, safe, nontoxic scratch-and-sniff feature.

Mo Smells Red, the first book in the series, has Mo smelling strawberries, roses and love itself. Cute in the extreme. A portion of the proceeds from the books go to help rescue animals find homes. Mo is going to be a star. Be ready for the appearance of Mo T-shirts in your children's lives.

Graphic novels were another big trend at BookExpo. As I learned, graphic novels are often neither graphic nor novel—they are adult versions of what we used to call comic books. NBM books was at the convention, along with local author David Seidman, who told me that Los Angeles has become fertile ground for the graphic novel, thanks to the abundance of animators and writers raised on comic books.

These days, comics range from humorous work to art of fantasy and the imagination, from children's comics to illustrated renderings of Proust and Kafka, from political cartooning to subversive alternative lit, from goth to Japanese manga.

Some of the most interesting books these days are being published by university presses, such as the university presses of Indiana, Nebraska, Michigan, Mississippi, Chicago, MIT,

Harvard, Princeton, and Yale, which publish everything from the hyperlocal, to the serious academic, to the just plain fun from all over the country. As just one example, Yale University is doing a series called American icons with titles such as Joseph Epstein writing about Fred Astaire.

Book Expo, however, was not just about free books. There were also speeches and panels (about books). *The New York Times*' Thomas Friedman spoke about how "green is the new red, white and blue," which not coincidentally is the title of Friedman's next book. There were author breakfasts with Philippa Gregory, Alec Baldwin, Chris Buckley, and Magic Johnson. There were also panels about film rights, bookselling and climate change, about Google and digital rights and digital editions, social networking, graphic novels, libraries, censorship, the Chinese market and the Chinese audience, the Latino audience and the panel I attended about—no surprise here—the Jewish audience.

A panel about the reading habits of Jewish Americans featured Stuart Matlins of Jewish Lights publishing house, Daisy Maryles of *Publishers Weekly* and Ruth Ellenson of the best-selling anthology, *The Modern Jewish Girls' Guide to Guilt.*

Panelists spoke of the importance of the Jewish Book Council run by Carolyn Starman Hessel, book clubs and synagogue book clubs. Matlins suggested that in his guesstimation, seventy percent of readers and more than seventy percent of book club attendees are women.

Ellenson, who has written for *The Jewish Journal* and whose book features an essay by *Jewish Journal* Religion Editor Amy Klein, told many humorous anecdotes about the pressures she faced to make her book less "Jewish." However, what Ellenson discovered was that what perhaps threatened to keep her from a mainstream audience helped her find a very loyal niche audience, Jewish readers who have supported her book in steady numbers since its publication.

No one who was in the room will ever forget when Ellenson told us the more "edgy title" one editor suggested for her book: *Burning Bushes.*

At one point, Carla Cohen, owner of Politics and Prose bookstore in Washington, DC, bemoaned the fact that there is not a contemporary version of *The Jewish Catalogue.* Several audience members then volunteered that they were the authors of soon-to-be-published books hoping to fill the gap, among them *Cool Jew* by Lisa Alcalay Klug (Andrews McMeel).

There was some question of if, and why, Jews buy a disproportionate number of books. Is it just a matter of education?

In some sense, this begged a question that nagged at the whole Book Expo: Whither books?

Is the book industry going the way of the music industry? Or the newspaper industry? Is digital the future? What percentage of the population will read books on their Kindle or other electronic devices or even on their Blackberry? If most nonfiction titles sell only 6,000 copies, how can such small sales support writers, editors, publishing companies?

The answer is, of course, no one knows, but stay tuned—or more to the point, keep reading.

Matlins had the best precis of the current marketplace: "The people who buy books," he opined, "are the people who buy books."

June 12, 2008

SANDLER AND THE ZOHAN

As everyone knows by now, Adam Sandler's *You Don't Mess With the Zohan* dives in where few comedies have gone before: The Middle East conflict between Arabs and Jews. Hollywood has a long tradition of preferring onscreen Jews to be Semitic-lite (or even better, portrayed by non-Jews such as Gregory Peck in *Gentleman's Agreement*).

Sandler, however, pulls no such punches in *Zohan*—Israel is Israel and Zohan's nemesis is a Palestinian terrorist—there is no attempt to create fake countries or nationalities. For that alone, Sandler and Sony, the studio that financed the film, should be commended.

As to whether *Zohan* will advance the cause of peace in the Middle East and increase regard for Israel and Israelis in the world at large, even as Israel itself celebrates its sixtieth anniversary, that's hard to say. But face it: Given the results of peace negotiations thus far over the last several decades under American, Israeli and Arab regimes of the right, left and center, "Zohan" stands as good a chance as any.

One thing's for sure. If the film's opening sequence on the beaches of Tel Aviv, featuring one fetching, toned, tanned hedonistic beach beauty after another (many of them tattooed), doesn't boost tourism to Israel, I don't know what will. At the very least, it will raise the bar on Israeli beauty (and when I say "bar," I mean Bar Rafaeli).

Mostly, watching *Zohan,* you will laugh. At times, you will be ashamed for doing so, given the crudeness or the simplicity of the joke, but you will laugh all the same (who knew hummus had so many uses and could be so funny?).

Sandler's Zohan, as you may know from the many ads and trailers, is Israel's greatest counterterrorism agent. Writing in *The New York Times,* A. O. Scott compared him to "a less anguished version of Eric Bana's character in *Munich*"—that may be so. (Although I was no fan of *Munich*—I just didn't find the movie that funny—I only laughed like twice.)

Zohan is unstoppable, undefeatable, a master of martial arts, able to catch a bullet with his fingers, punch through a wall, swim faster than a Jet Ski—you get the idea.

But he is tired of war, tired of the fighting, tired of being Israel's go-to guy for missions against terrorists. What he wants is to pursue his dream: to style hair to make men and women look "silky smooth." While on a mission to capture the notorious terrorist, "The Phantom" (John Turturro), he fakes his death.

Zohan then travels to New York, where he is no longer famous and is ridiculed for his eighties-style clothes, hairstyle and love of disco. A fellow Israeli recognizes him (Iddo Mosseri, an Israeli actor), and at his lowest moment, Zohan is tempted to join him working in an electronics store. But his friend warns him away, saying the lure of electronic sales is too strong; it kills dreams.

Zohan gets a job instead at a salon run by Dalia, a Palestinian, played by Emmanuelle Chriqui (of *Entourage* fame), on a Brooklyn street where one side is Arab, the other Israeli and everyone, although distrusting the other, gets along.

Zohan boosts Dalia's struggling business by showering his attentions on her elderly clientele, using a technique pioneered by Zero Mostel in *The Producers.* Disgusting and very funny.

All is good until Zohan is recognized by an Arab cab driver played by Rob Schneider, who rounds up his fellow Arab cab drivers. After first calling the Hezbollah hotline, which is out of service until negotiations break down again, they call the Phantom, now a successful fast-food operator in the Middle East, and tell him where Zohan works.

Along the way, *Zohan* is riddled with cameo performances and appearances by Shelley Berman, Lainie Kazan, Michael Buffer, Kevin James, Kevin Nealon, John McEnroe, Mariah Carey and even Los Angeles local luminaries, such as entertainment manager Guy Oseary, Academy of Motion Picture Arts and Sciences President Sid Ganis and Roni from Roni's Diner.

In the end, it turns out the bad guys are not the Israelis or Arabs but a Donald Trump-like developer who is pitting the Brooklyn Israeli and Arab residents against each other so that he can build a mall.

When the Phantom finally confronts Zohan in America, he confesses that he, too, has a dream: He wants to sell shoes, and Zohan encourages him, telling him that in the United States, Arabs and Israelis put aside their differences to live their dreams and get on with their lives.

A couple of weeks ago, at the press conference for *Zohan,* Mosseri and Schneider talked about how the Israeli and Arab actors at first were suspicious of each other but eventually came to have lunch together at what they dubbed *The Peace Table,* where they had long, personal and occasionally heated discussions on the Middle East, even as they developed friendships that culminated in a trip to Las Vegas. Only in America! (Perhaps the sequel should have Zohan pressed back into service to save Las Vegas during his bachelor party.)

The Zohan peace plan of living as Israelis and Arabs do in America has been dubbed by that well-known critic of Middle East policy, *Daily Variety*, as "simplistic." Maybe, but it is also very Sandler.

First and foremost, Sandler is an instinctual comedian. He looks to the nuggets from his own experience or belief system to fuel his comedies.

Born in 1966, Sandler is of a generation that has known Israel only as a superpower. As Sandler recounted at the *Zohan* press conference, as a kid, his impression was that Israel was this country that everyone wanted to destroy, but no one could—they kicked ass.

So there was a generational difference in perspectives: His parents worried about Israel's survival; Sandler thought Israel's ability to triumph was cool. That schism is presented in the movie, and I'm not sure I've ever seen it on the screen before. To write a think piece about Sandler may sound, at first, like a contradiction in terms—not unlike "jumbo shrimp" or "military intelligence"—but understanding who Sandler is and where he comes from goes a long way toward explaining his success.

Sandler was born in Brooklyn to Judy, a nursery school teacher, and Stanley, an electrical engineer, according to IMDB.com. At age five, the family moved to Manchester, NH.

Being Jewish in Manchester must have been a special experience, since it inspired the comic mind not only of Sandler but also fellow Manchester resident Sarah Silverman. It also seems to be have inspired Sandler's 2002 landmark venture into animation, *Eight Crazy Nights* (the first-ever feature animated Chanukah movie).

Sandler began performing stand-up comedy while at New York University. He also nabbed a recurring role on *The Cosby Show* in 1987 as Theo's friend, Smitty. Once on the comedy circuit, he moved to Los Angeles, where he roomed with Judd Apatow.

Dennis Miller recommended Sandler to Lorne Michaels, who hired him for *Saturday Night Live* in 1990. It was on *SNL* that Sandler first met both Schneider and Robert Smigel. And as Smigel revealed to my colleague, Jay Firestone, in these pages, Sandler's first *SNL* sketch was a spoof of Israeli hard sell, called *The Sabra Shopping Network*. It was written by Smigel, whom Sandler would tap to write *Zohan* with him and Apatow.

Sandler left *SNL* in 1995 to pursue a film career. *Billy Madison* and *Happy Gilmore,* for which he shared writing credit, followed soon thereafter, establishing Sandler's popularity. The 1998 film, *The Waterboy,* was Sandler's first to pass the $100 million mark, establishing him as a bankable comedy superstar.

Over the last decade, Sandler has produced or starred in more than a dozen films and shared writing credit on a handful. Yet if you ask most people, they hark back to the movies early in his career, such as *Happy Gilmore* or *The Wedding Singer,* as having cemented his image as a sweet, emotional, vulnerable cretin savant.

Yet many people I know between the ages of fifteen to thirty don't seem particularly interested in Sandler or in this movie. They tell me they used to like his movies—now they're not sure.

His humor, they say, seems too old-fashioned (I think the word they are looking for is schmaltzy).

The humor they like is more deadpan, like *The Office* or *Flight of the Conchords*. They like Apatow's movies, and although Apatow has a writing credit on this one, they perceive this movie as different.

I'm not worried for Sandler. As Sony is well aware, since *The Waterboy*, almost all the movies that Sandler produces and stars in perform reliably in the $120 million to $135 million range, according to Box Office Mojo, and often better, and that includes movies you might not think of as successful, such as *The Longest Yard* ($158 million), *I Now Pronounce You Chuck & Larry* ($120 million), *Click* ($137 million) and *Anger Management* ($135 million).

The only exception is *Little Nicky* ($39 million). In its first weekend, *Zohan* came in second in the box-office race, earning an estimated $40 million, behind only an animated panda.

That being said, it is important to point out some differences between the Apatow and Sandler oeuvres.

Apatow's movies are grounded in reality, fueled by embarrassing or awkward moments that have happened or could happen in real life. Many of the films associated with Apatow, such as his *Knocked Up* or Seth Rogen's *Superbad* or Jason Segal's *Forgetting Sarah Marshall* (co-produced by Apatow), feature nice Jewish boys who are ambition-challenged, pot-smoking and untoned (what's the opposite of "buff"?) but who get the girl—usually a far more beautiful girl than anyone would ever imagine they could win.

Zohan subverts this paradigm. Sandler's Zohan is a man's man—hairy, comfortable grilling fish in the nude (Apatow has made a crusade of male nudity, and this may be part of his contribution to *Zohan*). That being said, Zohan is no nebbish. He is used to being the best at everything and to being irresistible and so comfortable with himself that sex is just another physical prowess about which he is nonchalant (until he falls in love).

Dalia, the girl he falls in love with, is not unreachable, she's just not Jewish, and a Palestinian to boot. But given that she, too, is tired of the fighting—and even drinks Israeli soda—they fall in love, and in keeping with Hollywood traditions from *The Jazz Singer* on, his parents approve.

Speaking of parents, Sandler confessed that his own parents seem pleased with him. As Sandler made clear at the *Zohan* press conference, he was raised in a Jewish home. His wife is Jewish, his child is Jewish (at his wedding, Sandler's dog walked down the aisle wearing a kippah, so perhaps his dog is Jewish, as well).

Sandler's stance toward his Judaism seems much like Popeye's credo, "I am what I am." It is an attitude that has served him well.

Sandler's instinct that comedy was to be found in mocking Israeli stereotypes and the conflict between Arabs and Jews may not earn him an Oscar or the Nobel Peace Prize. But *Zohan* brings these topics to the mainstream in a way that will have many, many people laughing.

In this way, Sandler is hewing to a long Jewish tradition that has always chosen laughter over tears in the face of seemingly insolvable adversity. Funny, that.

June 12, 2008

THE HEART AND THE DRIVE

HATSCHEK BELA

Hatschek Bela.

The very sound of my great-grandfather's name brings a smile to my face.

In Hungarian, last names go first, so although Bela was his first name, he has always been Hatschek Bela to me—all one name—a legendary figure in our family, a celebrated forebear about whom my mother and grandmother told stories.

He was famous for being the first man in Hungary to own a car, and my grandmother kept a clipping from the Royal Hungarian Automobile Society with a picture of him seated at the controls of his Benz with a little girl on the rear rumble seat. Beneath the photo was the caption in Hungarian, German and French, proclaiming "Hatsek Bela le premier automobiliste Hongrois sur son voiture Benz en 1895."

The picture always fascinated me. My great-grandfather sits at the control of his open-air Benz looking, with his dark beard and mustache, like Sigmund Freud, smoking a cigar and wearing his homburg tilted at a rakish angle, as well as a suit—perfectly tailored to show his starched white cuffs. I also loved looking at the little girl sitting at the rear of the vehicle, gazing at the camera like a little doll in her pinafore and large hat—that was my grandmother, Adrienne, whom I only knew as an old woman.

Hatschek Bela had a Benz before Mercedes did. That was way cool.

My grandmother and mother used to tell stories about Hatschek Bela. From their stories, I took him to be debonair, slightly eccentric, with a healthy sense of humor.

Regarding the famous Benz, the story told in our family is that, one day, Hatschek Bela left on a trip. He disappeared for a few weeks, without anyone really knowing why or where he was going. When he returned, he did so with the vehicle—transported on a train in its own car. But wait—there's more: Hatschek did not return alone. He brought back a mechanic from Germany, as well, to care for it.

The car was a curiosity in Budapest. The most famous apocryphal story about Hatschek Bela and the car involves no less grand a personage than Austrian Emperor Franz Joseph. As the story goes, the emperor was visiting Budapest. He was standing on a balcony reviewing a parade when he heard a loud explosion—he hit the deck, fearing it was an assassination attempt. But someone said, "Don't worry, that's just Hatschek Bela in his car."

I once tried to research this story. All that I could confirm was that the Emperor Franz Joseph did visit Budapest as part of the 1896 celebration of 1,000 years of Hungary's nationhood.

However, it does seem possible that the emperor would be reviewing crowds, and that there would be a parade, and that the car would be shown off in some fashion.

Apocryphal or not, Hatschek and the emperor remain a good story, and who knows, it might even be true.

Hatschek Bela died when my mother was just a child. But she remembered him as handsome, always well dressed. And he was vain. He was interested in new inventions. He was fond of having family portraits taken—there is a story that he gave one to my grandmother. Inscribed on the back, it said: Who are these people?

My grandmother, Adrienne Hatschek Saar Morvai Bogner (she married several times), was the family archivist. She kept a leather portfolio filled with yellowing documents that held the birth, marriage and death records of her family. When she died, it passed to my mother, who really wasn't all that interested. But I was. So the portfolio came into my possession.

Here's where my research began. One day, several years ago, I sat down to sort through the documents that charted our family tree. From the crumbling yellow pages with handwritten entries, the story of my family emerged.

I learned that Hatschek Bela was born October 25, 1858, in Budapest, the son of Max (Miksa) Hatschek and Julia Boscovitz Hatschek. His father, Max, was a medical doctor, an optician. They lived at 13, Palatinus, in Pest—an address in the center of the city.

On July 4, 1886, a twenty-eight-year-old Hatschek, who by then had become an optician like his father, was married to Gizella Back. She was just seventeen, according the marriage certificate, the daughter of Fulop Back and Jeannette Reitzer Back.

They were married at the Dohány Temple in Budapest (Budapest's largest temple, akin to Temple Emmanuel in New York, or Wilshire Boulevard Temple in Los Angeles).

My mother always claimed that her great-grandfather, Fulop Back, had been rashe kol (head of the Jewish community in Budapest), and that he was a great rabbi. However, when I visited the Jewish Community Center in 2003, a list of Budapest's rashim kol does not include a Fulop Back. Furthermore, on Hatschek Bela's wedding certificate Fulop Back is listed as a merchant.

I found two possible explanations: The list of rashim kol in Budapest's Jewish Community Center does list a Jozef Boscovitz, who was president of the Jewish community between 1851 and 1858. As Hatschek Bela's mother's maiden name was Boscovitz, perhaps her father was rashe kol and my mother got the sides of the family wrong.

Another is that Fulop was related to Joseph Bach (1784-1866), an important Talmud teacher from Old Buda. He was the first preacher of the Jewish community of Pest, and the first to preach sermons in German rather than Yiddish.

In any event, this was the marriage of two members of Budapest's rising Jewish middle class. The evidence is that Dr. Mayer Kayserling married them at the Dohány Temple.

"Jewish Budapest: Monuments, Rites, History" (Central European University Press, 1999), explains that the Dohány Temple, which had been consecrated in 1859, a year after Hatschek's birth, was symbolic of the rise and self-importance of Pest's Jewish community and their intention to be fully integrated members of the Hungarian nation. The Dohány is a magnificent Moorish-style edifice that can hold 3,000 visitors, where

Budapest's version of Reform Judaism, called Neolog, was observed. Although the Dohány had a rabbi, Samuel Kohn, who delivered sermons in Hungarian, they also had Kayserling, who joined the temple in 1879 and was a German Jewish scholar. As subjects of the Austro-Hungarian Empire, the majority of the congregation still preferred their sermons in German. Kayserling remained with the Dohány until his death in 1905—long enough to see Hatschek Bela in his automobile.

The documents reveal that both Bela and his father, Max, were opticians, a fact that intrigued me. Turning again to "Jewish Budapest," I learned that one of the important early prominent figures in Budapest's Jewish history is Ignac Hirschler (1823-1891), a famous ophthalmologist. He was elected president of the Hungarian Jewish Congress in 1868-1869, was a member of the Hungarian Academy of Sciences, as well as a member of Hungary's Upper House of Government and president of the Jewish community. What direct or indirect influence Hirschler had on the Hatschek family is not known. But I wonder if it is just a coincidence that Max and Bela were opticians, too? Could they be related? Could Hatschek be a Hungarian (Magyarized) version of Hirschler? These are all questions I hope to further research one day.

Regardless, Hatschek Bela was not an eye doctor as much as a businessman. His stationery, a copy of which was sent to me by Hungarian journalist Pal Negyesi, indicates that he owned the "first Hungarian glass eye factory."

Although this may sound a bit odd today, eye injuries and lost eyes were much more common in the age of the sword fight, particularly before eye surgery and repair became more sophisticated. It was also an enterprise in which artistry was valued.

My mother recalled being taken to her grandfather's factory, which her Uncle Hugo ran. A sign with a giant eye hung outside, and my mother recalls finding it frightening—and memorable.

I also discovered that Hatschek Bela, or at least his factory, also made ocular equipment, such as binoculars. About three years ago, I received an e-mail out of the blue from a man who had purchased a pair on eBay. Upon Googling "Hatschek Bela" he had come across an article I had written and e-mailed me to ask for further details.

While writing this article, I decided to e-mail the man, and ask if he would consider selling me the binoculars. I can report that I am now the proud owner of a pair of World War I-era binoculars. They work, and they came with leather case lined with red silk. Stamped on the case's cover in bold gold letters is "Hatschek Bela," along with the address of his company store, located at 2 Vaci Utca (Budapest's most elegant shopping street—akin to Rodeo Drive or Fifth Avenue).

Hatschek Bela died on October 23, 1922 (his wife, Gizella Hatschek, died five years later). He had two children, Adrienne (my grandmother), born in 1892, and Hugo, born in 1895. He lived long enough to see Adrienne appear on stage, see her marry and to see his grandchild, Eva (my mother). He lived long enough to see Hugo become an optician and to know that his son would carry on his business. Adrienne lived in the family home and factory at 4 Munkas St. until her own marriage in 1915; Hugo continued to live there until it was taken over by the German SS in 1944.

In 2003, when I visited Budapest, I discovered that—in the records of the Jewish Community Center at 12 Sip Utca—

Hatschek Bela and Gizella are listed as having been buried at the Kozma Street Jewish cemetery. However, when I visited the cemetery, I could not find their graves. Someone suggested that perhaps someone else had been buried above them. That, too, is a mystery I hope to solve one day (I did find Hugo's grave in the Kozma Street cemetery).

At the same time, I also discovered that my great-great-grandmother, Jeannette Reitzer, Hatschek's mother-in-law, was born in 1849 in Altofen (Old Buda) and died in 1891 in Budapest. Like Dr. Kayserling and other members of the 19th century Budapest bourgeoisie, she is buried in the Salgótarjáni Utca Cemetery. When I visited the cemetery in 2003, I found her grave marker—a striking black obelisk.

To be able to trace my family's roots in Budapest back to 1849 was very meaningful. To imagine where their lives played out across centuries, to walk down those streets, to see buildings and synagogues and to be able to say my family walked these streets, my family members lived here, they were married in this place and buried here, it gives one a feeling that is larger than one's self—a connection between present and past, a feeling of history.

As for Hatschek Bela owning Hungary's first automobile, Pal Negyesi, a Hungarian freelance journalist who writes about automobile history, published an article in 2007 that tried to find a definitive answer to who had the first car in Hungary. He could not confirm anything.

As part of my own research, I e-mailed the picture of my great-grandfather in the Benz to Mercedes' own historians in Germany. They confirmed that it was a 1894 "Velo."

According to their records, in 1894 Benz launched the Velociped model—nicknamed Velo—a light vehicle that takes its place in history as the first small car and the first series-automobile in the world. The Velo had an engine that produced 1.5 horsepower at 450 revolutions per minute (according to their records, the engine's performance could be improved to 3.5 horsepower at 800 revolutions per minute). The Velo cost 2,000 marks in 1894.

However, Mercedes had no records of Hatschek Bela purchasing a Velo. Their records do indicate that in 1896, a year after the picture was taken, a Benz No. 375 was delivered to Hungary. No recipient is listed.

However, as our family lore has it, Hatschek traveled out of the country and returned with the car. Negyesi in his research turns up newspaper accounts from 1921 and 1967 anointing Hatschek as the first Hungarian automobilist, stating that "Hatschek learnt to drive a bit in Mannheim, Germany and Benz dispatched a ' driver' to Budapest, in order to help Hatschek learn how to properly drive and maintain his car."

This sounds very close to what I heard as a child and also leaves open the possibility that Hatschek purchased his car abroad from a dealer or a private party and then brought it home. One can certainly question who had the first car, but there is no doubt that Hatschek owned a Benz Velo, and that alone was a pretty remarkable occurrence at that time for anyone—but certainly for a Jewish citizen of Hungary (although who knows, he may have been dismissed by some as just another of the "nouveau riche" Jewish merchants corrupting Hungary with new ideas).

For me, I look at the picture of Hatschek Bela sitting in his Benz, his calm authority, his debonair charm, his comfort in being modern, his style, and imagine all that as part of my DNA.

Then, as if by magic, it happens again: I start to smile.

July 3, 2008

WAXING ROTH

The movie, *Elegy,* which opens August 8 and stars Ben Kingsley as David Kepesh and Penelope Cruz as the object of his desire, is the latest film to be adapted from the writings of Philip Roth. This one is based on his novella, *The Dying Animal.*

Despite Roth's long, successful career in American letters, his track record on film has been far spottier. Yet *Elegy,* directed by Isabel Coixet, who is Spanish, has created a certain buzz: Could it be that a woman, a European—albeit working in English—is what it takes to successfully translate Roth's work to film?

Let me get back to you on that. First, to set *Elegy* in context, I decided to watch every film adapted from Roth's work.

My mission started simply enough: a quick search on imdb.com turned up a succinct list of eight works on film and TV, stretching back to the 1950s.

Some had never been released on video, some are only in VHS, some were available at the local video store, some had to be tracked down in specialty shops or in university or museum archives. My quest led me across Los Angeles and afforded me the pleasure of visiting some of the city's most beautiful libraries and research facilities, as well as some of its best-stocked video stores.

In 1960, Roger Corman produced *The Battle of Blood Island,* which was adapted from a 1958 short story that ran in Esquire titled, *Expect the Vandals.* Shot in black and white and only 64 minutes long, *Blood Island* is part of a trilogy of films Corman made in Puerto Rico.

Netflix carries this film as a DVD double feature, paired with a non-Roth film called, *Shell Shock* (that has nothing to do with Roth). Locally, *Blood Island* can't be found at Blockbuster, the Santa Monica or Los Angeles public libraries or such local rare video sources as CineFile or Vidiots.

So, I turned to my video store of last resort, Eddie Brandt's Saturday Matinee on Tujunga Avenue in North Hollywood, a shop whose eccentric and extensive film collection rarely disappoints.

It was there that I found one lonely DVD of the film. The story is set on an island in the South Pacific, where two American soldiers, Moe and Ken, are the only survivors of an attack on Japanese forces and are forced to hide out and get along. Moe is a thirty-five-year-old Jewish accountant, with a wife and kids back home, who sprinkles his conversation with Yiddish expressions. Ken, who was injured in the attack and whom Moe must take care of (but resents doing so) is a younger, more naive, all-American kid. Moe is not very likeable, but we understand his predicament. At one point, Ken, pushed to the end of his rope, makes an anti-Semitic jab at Moe. We know Ken didn't really mean it, but Moe feels Ken's comment justifies his worldview.

In the end, the two are rescued—just before the island is to be used as a nuclear test site. The film is more a character study than anything else, and our feelings about Moe are left unresolved. Nonetheless, Moe represents an early proto-Roth protagonist, one who has not yet moved beyond ethnic identity, but remains plenty angry.

Roth's next adaptation to film appeared in October 1960, when *The Contest for Aaron Gold,* originally published in 1955 as a short story in EPOCH, appeared as an episode of the television series, *Alfred Hitchcock Presents.*

I first turned to the Paley Center for Media's library, but they did not have a copy. They directed me to the UCLA Film & Television Archive, which had a copy that I was allowed to screen only in the media lab of UCLA's Powell Library. The special treat here was Powell Library, which stands across from Royce Hall on the UCLA campus and is worth visiting just for the beauty of its main reading room.

The Contest for Aaron Gold is noteworthy because its Philip Roth-esque lead is played by the recently deceased Sydney Pollack, who turns in a credible performance as a sculptor who has taken a job as the ceramics instructor at a summer camp. In the film, all the characters have Jewish last names, but there is no mention of the place being a Jewish summer camp, or of the campers or the counselors being Jewish. But there is some tension here between the lead character trying to stand up for his artistic beliefs and not cave in to the pressures of the man running the place—some of the issues around money and career that arise later in *Goodbye, Columbus. The Contest* ends with a twist suitable for Alfred Hitchcock. As a one-hour episodic TV drama, albeit a slightly obvious and gimmicky one, I found it satisfying and enjoyable.

Almost a decade passed before the next Roth work turned up on the screen. By the time it did, Roth had become celebrated, and somewhat notorious, for both his first collection of short stories, *Goodbye, Columbus,* which came out in 1959, and for *Portnoy's Complaint,* published in 1968. Both were made into films, and both star Richard Benjamin.

Goodbye, Columbus, released in 1969, launched the careers of both Benjamin and Ali McGraw. This film was easy to find; a copy was readily available at the Santa Monica Public library.

Watching *Goodbye, Columbus* at half a century's remove from the short story's original publication is a strange experience. I found myself as ambivalent about Benjamin's Neil Klugman as he was about the Patimkin family. To me, the Klugmans and the Patimkins each seemed to be playing out their own strategy for rising above their immigrant backgrounds: One sought insulation from the evils of the world in books, the others in business and material goods. I found it hard to be judgmental, because I found them so much more alike than different.

McGraw's Brenda Patimkin was a far more sympathetic character than I recalled. Klugman, by contrast, never really seemed to care for Brenda beyond his desire for her (a trait common to Roth characters that would be examined in greater detail in *Portnoy*). In the original reviews, the film was praised for its naturalism and its humor, but from the twnty-first century perspective, I found it a less than satisfying experience.

Portnoy's Complaint was published in 1968 to huge acclaim. The 1972 film, written, produced and directed by Ernest Lehman, was considered a huge failure. Lehman was the screenwriter of such classics as *North by Northwest, Sweet Smell of Success, West Side Story, The Sound of Music, Sabrina* and *Who's Afraid of Virginia Woolf—Portnoy* is the only film he ever directed.

Watching the movie today, it struck me as yes, failed, but better than its reputation. Lehman chose to take what was in essence a comic monologue and set it as both a story of a love affair and of one man's attempt to heal himself via analysis of his relationships. At the same time, Lehman attempted to show the freedom that the sexual revolution inspired and the consequences of that freedom. Karen Black gives a very strong performance as "the monkey," and Richard Benjamin delivers a more nuanced performance than he gave in *Goodbye, Columbus.*

Another twelve years passed before PBS offered up a version of Roth's *The Ghost Writer* as part of its American Masters series in 1984. As far as I can tell, this is the only production for which Roth is credited with collaborating on the script. That may have something to do with the fact that Claire Bloom, whom Roth was then involved with, plays a role in the production.

I had imagined that a copy of this would be at UCLA or available on DVD or VHS, or even offered at Eddie Brandt. But it wasn't. Luckily, it was in the collection of the Paley Center, and I was able to screen it in their library.

Mark Linn-Baker, best known as Benjy Stone in *My Favorite Year* (and who would later gain a measure of cultural currency on the sitcom, *Perfect Strangers*) plays the young Nathan Zuckerman, a writer at the start of his career visiting Lonoff, a famous older writer, at Lonoff's country home on the very occasion when Lonoff's wife (Claire Bloom) leaves, and a much younger woman, his former student, urges Lonoff to run off with her. Zuckerman, whose parents and rabbi have rebuked him for the way he portrays Jews in his work, imagines the young woman to be Anne Frank, an Anne who survived the war and is now going to marry him.

Although tension-filled, *The Ghost Writer* unfolds at a somewhat leisurely pace, making the film perhaps not the most exciting adaptation of Roth's work, though certainly one of the most successful, conveying a measure of his writing's literary texture.

Twenty years passed after the PBS version of *The Ghost Writer* before another Roth novel made it to the screen. In the interim, Roth experienced a second wind as a novelist unparalleled in American letters, during which he won almost every major prize and award available to him, including the National Book Critics Award, the Pulitzer Prize and the Pen Faulkner award, among many others. If he were an athlete, you would have him checked for steroids. In this new era, almost everything he wrote was optioned, including *The Human Stain.*

The Human Stain (2003), which stars Anthony Hopkins and Nicole Kidman, was the easiest of Roth's films I sought out—Blockbuster had many copies—but it is probably the least successful adaptation of his work.

I will offer here that I once tried to option *The Human Stain* myself, but was outbid. My thought was to treat it as a murder mystery in which the detective uncovers a secret he had not bargained for. The hoped-for casting was Paul Newman (his agent when approached said, "Bring me an offer") and Ellen Barkin. So perhaps I am biased, but I believe that *The Human Stain* is a miss—whether you blame it on the casting or for being too faithful to the novel's exposition, the story just doesn't work on screen. The most poignant moments of the novel do not resonate.

Still, watching *The Human Stain* the other night, I was struck by how Roth weaved elements of the personal dramas of Anatole Broyard, who like Roth's hero, reached great heights while leaving his African American heritage behind, and R. B. Kitaj, who blamed his wife's death on those who attacked him—all the while setting this against the backdrop of the Monica Lewinski affair and the Clinton impeachment investigation.

Which brings us up to *Elegy.* David Kepesh, played by Ben Kingsley, is a teacher, a public intellectual. The movie opens with his appearance on Charlie Rose, and he is set up as a man beyond romantic love, an intellectual's Hef, who finds his romance in promiscuity. So, naturally, he is caught off-guard when he falls in love with one of his students, Consuela, a woman thirty years his junior. And when he does, he becomes so obsessively convinced that he will lose her, sooner or later, that he sabotages the relationship. There is also a further irony, an inside joke, almost, for those who know Roth's work, because Kepesh, who venerates Consuela's breasts, is also the protagonist of an earlier Roth work, *The Breast.*

Cruz is shot so lovingly in this film, it is hard to believe that she would not entrance anyone. Her work in the films of Pedro Almodóvar have demonstrated her incredible range and talents as an actress, but Coixet provides Cruz her greatest acting opportunity thus far in an English-language film (at least, that is, until Woody Allen's *Vicky Cristina Barcelona*).

Coixet also manages to soften the hard edge of Kepesh's narcissism, that same edge that one feels in other films made from Roth's work, such as *Portnoy.* Here, we understand how a man of a certain position, of a certain age, manages his private life with both a woman with whom he has had a long affair (played by Patricia Clarkson) and a younger woman.

I will not reveal the twist in the plot, and the denouement of the relationship, but intellectually it is powerful. Unfortunately, it is not as powerful on screen.

In the end, *Elegy* likely will not stand as the best adaptation of Roth's work. Roth's work continues to appeal because of the restless desire of his protagonists and the way he sets their stories against the backdrops of a given time and a given moment in his protagonist's life, as well as the way his character's sex drive acts as his life force. Roth continues to ask: If none of us get out alive, how do we go forward? And when we do, what do we make of this life and our loves?

As I write this, several of Roth's other works remain under option, including *American Pastoral,* as well as his forthcoming novel, *Indignation,* to be published in September by Houghton Mifflin. Perhaps one of them will transcend its provenance, to be remembered as a great film. But for that, we must still wait—and watch.

July 24, 2008

GREAT AS GOLD

Herbert Gold, who at eighty-four is among the elder statesmen of the Beat Generation, has a new book out, his twenty-eighth, a memoir titled *Still Alive! (A Temporary Condition).*

It is not an autobiography so much as a series of recollections of encounters with people who have been part of his life—neighbors, friends, family, lovers.

"I didn't really want to write my history." Gold said recently. "What impelled this book—what I wanted to do—was a meditation on age and the changes that happen and memories that happened."

What I found striking about *Still Alive* is that Gold often writes about people whom it is clear he didn't like much.

"People who have an impact on your life are often people you don't like," Gold told me when I mentioned this.

Fair enough. So we proceeded to talk about Gold's life and some of the people he has known along the way, as well as the books he has written.

Gold was born in 1924 in Cleveland, Ohio, a city he often calls, "The Paris of Northeastern Ohio," and he was raised in

Lakewood, a suburb where his next-door neighbor gave him his first taste of anti-Semitism. Not that the observance of Judaism interested him. Although Gold went to synagogue, he didn't like the rabbi and never became a bar mitzvah.

After graduating high school, he spent a year hitchhiking around the country, taking odd jobs, writing poems. His parents wanted him to stay in Cleveland and attend college there and then go on to medical school. Instead, he was accepted at Columbia College in New York, where he went with the ambition of being a writer.

It was at college that he first met Allen Ginsberg.

"He was seventeen. He was a bit crazy, and he was more eccentric than I was," Gold said.

They became friends, and Ginsberg soon surrounded himself with what would become known as The Beat Generation. Gold disagreed with Ginsberg about two things: one was Ginsberg's conviction that Gold should become a homosexual ("Ginsberg was a proselytizer," Gold said), and the other was Jack Kerouac, who was a football player then—not a writer. Gold did not like him.

"I crossed the street to avoid him," Gold said.

He also said that he knew even then that Kerouac was an anti-Semite (as Kerouac revealed himself to be in his last days), and he cites Ginsberg's affection for Kerouac as an example of Ginsberg's ability "to forgive people's sins."

A Fulbright Fellowship sent Gold to Paris, where he finished his first novel, launched his literary career and became friends with Saul Bellow.

In *Still Alive!* Gold draws an amusing and insightful portrait of the pleasures and difficulty of friendship with Bellow, young and old.

When Gold's first marriage, to Edith Zubrin, ended in divorce, he found himself in tough economic straits, he recalled. In our conversation, Gold said that although his first wife "was not a good person," he still felt terribly bereft when he recently learned that she had died.

To pay child support (they had two daughters, Ann and Judith), he became "the writing factory."

Gold wrote for Playboy and its imitators, publications with names such as Dude, Gent, Nugget and Coronet—not always using his real name. As he recalled, *Playboy* paid well—"with a feature inside the magazine, you could buy a VW, and with a lead feature you could buy a VW convertible."

He moved around the country, spending the winter in Florida—"you could rent an apartment in South Beach on Collins for two dollars a week; two dollars and fifty cents with air conditioning." He spent time in South Carolina, in New York, even back in Cleveland, where he edited a listings publication titled "What, Where, When." He took odd jobs; he taught at colleges and universities.

Eventually, he said, "I was able to dig myself out of that hole."

Gold settled in San Francisco just in time for a front-porch view of the sixties.

"I had a wonderful time," Gold recalled of the era. "There was a loosening of the barrier between the sexes, which has endured. Popular music became more interesting. There was a lot of fun being had. And fun is not to be derogated."

Gold explained that part of why hippie culture flourished "was economic. People could really make out without much."

But in *Still Alive!* Gold casts a jaundiced eye at some of what he calls "the nutty" aspects of the times, such as "the idiot radicals, those who thought the Cultural Revolution in China was a great thing."

In the book, Gold speaks of one friend explaining that it couldn't be bad, given that "it's Culture and it's a Revolution."

One of the reasons that Gold has tremendous affection for the '60s is because that was when he met his second wife, Melissa Dilworth, just around the time *Fathers,* his most successful novel, was published (*Fathers* finally afforded Gold some measure of financial security).

Gold writes very movingly of Melissa, the mother of his children Nina, Ari and Ethan. She is very present in *Still Alive* and his love for her still feels keen.

In the book, however, Gold describes how one couple kept encouraging Melissa to leave him to forge her own identity. Gold describes how all the marriages around them came apart, with the women running off, until their own marriage, like the last in a series of dominoes, fell.

"The idea that friends of ours could propagandize for our divorce" still rankles Gold.

Yet in our conversation, Gold also spoke of his wife's "restlessness" as being the chief cause of their marriage's dissolution.

Whatever the reason, he remained close with her and had made plans for them to have lunch for her birthday in 1991, when he learned that she had died in a helicopter crash with the man she was going to marry, concert promoter Bill Graham, whose foundation she had run.

The other great love of Gold's life has been Haiti, which he has traveled to on and off over the last five decades—a heartbreaking story that Gold told me "just gets worse and worse."

Strangely enough it was in Haiti that an Israeli, Shimon Tal, made it a Jewish place for him.

Gold's Jewish adventures in Haiti are described in his book *My Last Two Thousand Years,* which I also read in preparation for meeting Gold. It is a wonderful, moving book that describes the journey by which he embraced his Jewish identity, a book he told me he wanted to call *Being and Becoming.* Gold speaks movingly about the anti-Semitism he encountered as a child in Lakewood and in his early professional life; about the way people danced on the streets of the Upper West Side the night Israel became a State (although he and his first wife, being "internationalists," didn't see the point of creating new countries), and how he changed his mind and embraced the Jewish state in visits to Israel in 1958, on the occasion of its tenth anniversary, and shortly after the Six-Day War in 1967.

Gold has been a prolific writer of novels, short stories and nonfiction. In addition to *Fathers,* his novels include *Salt, She Took My Arm As If She Loved Me, The Man Who Was Not With It* and, one of my favorites, *A Girl of Forty,* which I recently reread.

A Girl of Forty holds up, but like many a novel one returns to, I found reading it now a different experience. Originally I was entranced by the portrait of Suki, the free-spirited woman at the center of the novel. Today, I read the novel more as a cautionary tale of the checks that became due after the sixties, and about coming to peace with the casualties caused.

Gold's reportage has included books on Biafra (*Biafra Goodbye*); his book on Haiti (*Best Nightmare on Earth*); and that republic of the soul, Bohemia and its earthly manifestations as chronicled by Gold (*Bohemia: Where Art, Angst, Love and Strong Coffee Meet*).

Over the years, as "writer in residue," as Gold calls it, at several colleges he has known or befriended many other writers of note. At Cornell he taught and knew Richard Farina and Thomas Pynchon. At SUNY Binghamton he was a teaching colleague of a young Richard Price. Although he is no name-dropper, the list of writers Gold has known is as wide as it is varied. During our conversation, there were few names that came up that Gold did not have an anecdote about (and usually a good one).

Gold is fit, spry and looks younger than his eighty-four years; he spoke with me at his son Ari's apartment. Gold may be an "old guy" (his term) but he remains as much a bohemian and a beatnik as he was when those terms were batted around more regularly.

As our time together ran out, I reminded Gold that *Fathers* told the story of an eighty-year-old father visiting his son, a father who declares that he's "still alive"—and here was Gold, at eighty-four, at the home of one of his sons, having written a memoir by the same name. What perspective did he now enjoy that he didn't then?

He said that back then, he regarded his father as old, in a way that his children didn't with him, in part because of his good health, but also because he had stuck to a bohemian way of dress and life. Also his father wasn't so supportive of Gold's artistic ambitions, while he fully supports the aspirations of his children, mentioning that his sons, Ari and Ethan, are both artists. (Ari and Ethan are in a band, The Honey Brothers, which also features Entourage star Adrian Grenier on drums; and Ari is the producer, director and star of the independent feature, *The Adventures of Power,* which, based on its trailer, appears to be a *Napoleon Dynamite*-ish tale of an air-drumming competition).

In the afterword to *Still Alive!*" Gold writes, "these pages are about love and memory, about why both are blessings and sorrows and a form of immortality."

At the start of our conversation, Gold had said to me that the concept of an afterlife "is very weak among Jews. We must make our heaven on our earth."

Immortality, Gold said, comes in the form of our children and our children's children. And for writers, in wanting their books to last. By all those standards, Herbert Gold is not only *Still Alive!*—he's immortal.

August 13, 2008

THE BROAD THEATER LANDS

Located at the intersection of 11th St. and Santa Monica Blvd., a striking modern building designed by Santa Monica architect Renzo Zecchetto sits on the site of a former elementary school playground and looks to have risen out of the ground sui generis, almost as if the Starship Enterprise had decided to dock in the middle of a residential city block.

It didn't.

This is the remarkable new Santa Monica College Performing Arts Center, comprised of the Eli and Edythe Broad Stage, a 499-seat state-of-the art theater, and the Edye Second Space, a ninety-nine seat "black box" theater. The new center, generally known as, simply, the Broad Stage, will debut with a gala opening on September 20 celebrating the life, career and music of Barbara Cook, the incomparable interpreter of the American Songbook.

For the theater-bereft Westside, whose residents once could only hope to see major theatrical productions by traveling downtown—often in rush hour—this is a big step up culturally. And it has been in development for a very long time—each detail dissected, discussed and considered.

The story goes that about ten years ago, Dale Franzen, an opera singer and, at the time, a member of Santa Monica College's music faculty, found herself at a dinner party with Dustin Hoffman, who once upon a time attended SMC. They met at the home of Piedad Robertson, then SMC's president, and talked about how great it would be if the Westside had a world-class performing arts center. So they sketched out a plan on a napkin. In time, as their vision took flight, Franzen took on the role of artistic director (she is now director), and Hoffman, who chaired the building committee, became chair of the Broad Stage's artistic advisory board.

Over the ensuing decade, a whole host of notables were consulted on making the dream a reality, including professionals associated with the Los Angeles Opera, the Los Angeles Chamber Orchestra, the Wiltern Theatre, Thousand Oaks Civic Arts Plaza and California Institute of the Arts. The old joke would have you believe that a donkey is a horse built by committee, yet in the case of the Santa Monica Performing Arts Center, Franzen managed to birth a butterfly from a silkworm (and I now officially have run out of species clichés).

Recently, Denise Leader Stoeber, associate director of the Broad Stage, gave me a tour of the facility as workers were putting on the finishing touches.

The Broad Stage was designed to be performer and audience friendly; the 499-seat theater space has a bright and clean design, yet feels intimate. Every seat affords clear sight lines meant to allow eye contact with the performers, and the seats themselves, imported from Italy, are firm and comfortable with good legroom (I tested them).

The stage was conceived to accommodate drama, dance and musical performances. Accordingly, there are thirty-seven fly lines, allowing for complex changes of scenery. There's also an orchestra pit, and the stage can accommodate a forty-five piece orchestra. A nine-foot concert Steinway piano, stored in its own specially designed cupboard, was a gift from donors Eva and Marc Stern. The stage flooring is partially sprung, so has a very good surface for dance, added to which a professional dance floor has been fashioned to be placed on top for performances.

Of course, the audience will see only a small part of the story. There is ample wing space, a comfortable green room, dressing rooms for solo performers as well as for a company of as many as fourteen. There's an orchestra lift and a trap pit that allows the stage to open from almost anywhere, and both the backstage and below-stage areas are handicap accessible. The Broad Stage also has a state-of-the-art sound system and state-of-the-art performance lighting (with two lighting bridges and follow spot room). It can accommodate filming as well as live broadcasts. As for screening movies or events—such as high-definition transmissions of live opera—the stage has both the sound system and the screen, though it still lacks the projector (donation, please?).

Finally, the acoustics were designed by Mark Holden of Jaffe-Holden Acoustics, who has worked with both the Kennedy Center in Washington, DC, and Lincoln Center in New York. A motorized variable acoustic drapery system allows the room to accommodate the sounds of different artistic performances and disciplines.

And for my green-conscious friends, eco-warriors please note: The theater was built with Honduran mahogany, a renewable resource, and the heating and cooling systems are beneath the floor and vent beneath the seats, rather than from above, while the lobby has been configured to be naturally vented, all for maximum efficiency.

Last, but by no means least, for those patrons who have had the experience of missing part of a performance because they were waiting in line outside a restroom, the good news is there are four public restrooms, and the main women's restroom includes a lounge and double capacity facilities.

The Edye Second Space, which is adjacent to the Broad Stage, is a ninety-nine seat theater, with its own lighting grid and the ability to show video. It is intended to showcase a wider range of more experimental works, including readings, plays and interdisciplinary productions.

For both the Broad Stage and the Edye, Stoeber said, the ambition is to be a place where artists used to performing before large audiences can perform in a more intimate setting, where new work can be incubated, and where new artists can be presented. To that end, for example, on October 11 the acclaimed mezzo-soprano Frederica von Stade will perform Mozart, Bernstein and Poulenc, as well as new works composed for her by composer and accompanist Jake Heggie.

Just to give you a sense of what architect Renzo Zecchetto has accomplished, in its technical abilities the Broad Stage is at the same level as UCLA's Royce Hall, yet Royce can hold an audience three times as large. The combination of the intimacy of the Broad and the technical virtuosity is unparalleled here.

What is remarkable, when you think about it, is that until now, no such performing arts center for music, dance, and theater has existed west of the 405 Freeway. That is not to say that the Westside has been without temples of culture: The Getty Center and the Getty Center Malibu have staged theater events, readings and happenings, as has the Hammer Museum in Westwood, and there have been events at Bergamot Station in Santa Monica; the relatively new Kirk Douglas Theatre in Culver City (an outpost of the downtown Center Theatre Group), has mounted significant theater productions; as has the Miles Playhouse in Reed Park. Santa Monica Civic Auditorium hosts the occasional concert, and the Skirball has, among other offerings, a thriving world music program. Nonetheless, despite these and many other performance spaces, the Westside has never had a dedicated stage of this caliber to attract world-class artists.

To ensure that Los Angeles denizens can enjoy their evening, the Broad Stage parking lot can accommodate 289 cars, in addition to valet parking, fitting, since as David Mamet reportedly said of the new venue, "the only thing more important than a forum where the community can go hear the truth is a forum where the community can go to hear the truth with adequate parking."

What then, you may ask, is the price tag for a world-class arts center? More than you might imagine: $45 million. And if you are a resident of Santa Monica or Malibu, you can thank yourself for making all this possible: In 2004 Santa Monica and Malibu passed a $35 million bond measure to support the project; $5 million came from other government agencies and individual donors, along with additional funds from a 2002 bond measure passed to finance improvements to Santa Monica College.

This marriage of public and private funds and of a community college and a performing arts center with world-class ambitions required a fair amount of creative collaboration and innovation in of itself.

"Embedded in the original Santa Monica College charter is the call for a performing arts center, so the stage fulfills our mandate and our traditions," said Chui. L. Tsang, the current president of Santa Monica College. One can also point to KCRW-FM, the nationally renowned radio station that broadcasts from the SMC campus, as an analogous "community service" of SMC.

In practice, what this means is that the college will use the space for rehearsing its orchestra, college band and chorus (which can include as many as a hundred people), and for performances associated with those groups. The Madison Building behind the center is available for classes and for rehearsals, as is the Edye Second Space.

Both the Broad Stage and the Edye will plan their programming around the college's use. At the same time, the Madison Group, a nonprofit organization created to stand at arms-length from the college, will lease the space and administer other programming for the center while raising money for what Stoeber called "this world-class programming in a world-class building." Memberships are available, and the inaugural season package has a five-ticket-for-the-price-of-four deal.

The inaugural season offers evenings of song, dance, music and theater from a diverse group of artists, ranging from mezzo-soprano Von Stade on opening night (October 11) to jazz artist Theo Bleckmann, cajun ensemble The Pine Leaf Boys and a cappella group Chanticleer, to dance companies such as Lulu Washington and Diavolo, musicians Lee Ritenour and Dave Grusin, as well as conductor Kent Nagano leading soloists from the Montreal Symphony (for a full schedule of events go to TheBroadStage.com).

The first season, impressive as it is, is still somewhat of a "soft launch," as they call it in the Internet world. Given that the opening is about a year behind schedule, the artists for the first season needed a certain flexibility to accommodate the Broad Stage. As Franzen has noted, the first season performances "allow us to test how the room and our systems perform in staging music, oratory, song and drama." The second season is already being scheduled, and there is talk of including more ethnic dance and more family offerings. Hoffman has been working on theater offerings to launch next year.

To support the programming as well as arts education, Eli and Edythe Broad donated $10 million to create an endowment. At a press conference earlier this year to announce the gift, Broad proclaimed: "We have the Walt Disney Concert Hall in downtown Los Angeles and now the Westside will have its own premier performing arts venue."

That the Broads have become our modern Medicis was not lost on Hoffman, who lauded them: "Without people like the Broads, we wouldn't have commissioned work of Mozart and Bach and Beethoven and so many of the great painters. How they use their capital is commendable."

Initially the Broads had urged that the theater be named after Hoffman, but they were ultimately persuaded otherwise. "Edye loves the theater" press materials quote Broad as saying, "and after fifty-three years of marriage, I wanted to honor her by naming the second space "The Edye.""

As for Hoffman, during the planning of the Broad Stage, one of his suggestions was to have a restroom just off-stage for performers—apparently his many years in the theater have taught him that such a contrivance would be invaluable. The restroom is now there, and Hoffman has asked that a plaque noting his contributions to the Broad Stage be placed there.

Something about that just tickles me. The Broads may have their names on the front of the building, but Hoffman has created his own rung on Rambam's ladder: the ironic acknowledgement.

The Broad Stage, as it goes forward, will no doubt evolve. As part of Santa Monica College and as part of the Santa Monica community, it has a rare opportunity to make its "global theater" locally relevant. The degree to which it becomes integral to the community and to Los Angeles as a whole will depend on both the quality and choice of the offerings, as well as its responsiveness to the audience. A task that poses as many questions as it does challenges.

For example, given that Emeritus College is also part of Santa Monica College, serving the senior community, will the Broad Stage create programs suited to senior schedules when the facility is otherwise not in use? Similarly, what about family programs? Will there be the equivalent of "early bird specials"? Weekend afternoon shows at family-friendly hours? Will they hew to the classic, or tilt to the new, or provide both? And how will the audience respond? (And who will they be?) All this remains to be seen.

For now, let us rejoice in the fall harvest of riches in Santa Monica: from newly opened restaurants, such as R+D Kitchen on Montana and Anisette just off the Third Street Promenade, to the forthcoming relocation of Santa Monica Seafood and the café and oyster bar they intend to open, to the imminent arrival of Diesel Bookstore in the Country Mart, and to this new starship that docked on 11th Street (with ample parking), ready to take all who enter on voyages of the heart, mind, soul and spirit.

September 11, 2008

DEFENDER OF FAITH

If the bestseller charts are any indication, it's become popular to condemn religion.

Books such as Sam Harris' *Letter to a Christian Nation* and *The End of Faith,* Richard Dawson's *The God Delusion,* Christopher Hitchens' *God Is Not Great* and Bill Maher's soon-to-be-released film, *Religulous,* would have us see faith as antiquated, illogical and dangerous.

And let's face it, the arguments they make are not without merit: In the shadow of September 11, religion seems at the root of much hatred and violence the world over. The announcement of a financial, sexual or political scandal involving a religious official—whether we cringe or feel some secret schadenfreude—no longer shocks us. At the same time, in this country as in others, it seems like religion is increasingly seeking to take on public and political dimensions, reaching into education, medicine, science and social programs.

In a world where religion is the cause of so much folly, it becomes harder to defend faith, which makes Rabbi David Wolpe's new book, *Why Faith Matters* (HarperOne), all the more important.

Why Faith Matters is not a book that will convince anyone who doesn't already believe in God—nor is it meant to. Yet believer and nonbeliever alike should find *Why Faith Matters* thought-provoking and challenging.

What the book does well, in short, succinct chapters, is address some of the more popularly held charges leveled against religion, such as "religion causes violence" or "science and religion are at odds." And it does so in a readable and erudite way, quoting from sources as diverse as Tacitus, Heinrich Heine, Nietzsche and Rabbi Hayyim of Zans.

More importantly, it makes the case for the seldom-acknowledged benefits of faith, such as community and charity, and elucidates how religion and religious practice can enhance the lives even of those who don't and will never believe in God. Wolpe also hopes the book will give comfort to those who have faith.

"It's not only written for those who doubt," Wolpe said recently, "but to settle the souls of people who believe."

Wolpe is turning fifty this Friday, September 19, and has been the rabbi at Sinai Temple in Los Angeles for the past eleven years. *Why Faith Matters* is his sixth book, and he wrote it not as a polemic response to the *New Atheists,* but as a personal book about his own journey.

He was born in Harrisburg, Pa., where his father, Gerald Wolpe, was a Conservative rabbi. When David was ten, the family moved to Philadelphia, when Wolpe's father became the rabbi of Har Zion, a large Conservative synagogue on the city's Main Line.

Stephen Fried's *The New Rabbi* (Bantam 2002) chronicled the search to find a replacement for Wolpe's father when he retired. A *New York Times* article about the book describes Wolpe's relationship with his father as "wonderfully complicated."

In *Why Faith Matters,* Wolpe explains that as a teenager, after seeing the vivid documentary footage about the Holocaust in Alain Resnais' *Night and Fog,* he became an atheist, embracing Bertrand Russell as one of his sages. Wolpe said he is attempting in this book to speak to his younger self. Yet, to a great extent, Wolpe now regards atheism as a failure of the imagination.

His central argument boils down to a rejection of the notion that "the only thing that is real is what you see or measure." Faith, he argues, adds another dimension to our experience of the world.

To Wolpe, religious faith is "an orientation of the universe," a way to invest all we do and all we experience with wonder and with meaning. When Peggy Lee asks: "Is that all there is?" Wolpe answers, "No."

This reminded me of an incident that occurred when my daughter was very young. She went through a phase, as all children do, of looking at the world around her, full of questions.

One night she asked me who made the stars in the sky. I replied, "God did," as much to come up with a quick and final answer as to avoid giving a more complicated scientific one.

A few weeks later, coming home late, as my wife, daughter and I stood at the front door, and as I fumbled to find my keys, my daughter said: "Listen." I listened and didn't hear anything.

"What?" I asked. She pointed upward and said, "It's The God. The God is everywhere."

Many people don't see or hear God's presence at all. And some feel that believing is childish.

Wolpe believes, however, that "there are things we outgrow and things we grow into." That struck me. What we dismiss as young people (like the value of having a job with a health care plan or retirement fund), we might revisit as we grow older.

Wolpe's own journey led him after graduating from the University of Pennsylvania from teenage atheist to studying to become a rabbi at the University of Judaism (UJ) in Los Angeles (now American Jewish University). He spent a year in Israel and was ordained in 1987 at the Jewish Theological Seminary (JTS) in New York, where he wrote his first book, *The Healer of Shattered Hearts* (Henry Holt & Company).

Over the next few years, Wolpe bounced back and forth between Los Angeles and New York, serving as director of UJ's library and assistant to the chancellor of JTS before returning finally to Los Angeles to serve as rabbi at Sinai Temple. Although Wolpe has been Sinai's rabbi for the last eleven years, he has performed High Holy Day services at Sinai since he was a student twenty-five years ago.

His tenure has not been without controversy. Whether it's been making peace among his diverse congregants or addressing the allegorical nature of Scripture or encouraging "rock" services, such as Craig Taubman's *Friday Night Live* (which can draw as many as 1,000 attendees to services with gospel, hip-hop or rock music and speakers from Elie Wiesel to writer David Kohan of *Will & Grace*), Wolpe's tenure has been marked by a certain fearlessness.

He brings the same approach to his brief in defense of faith, embracing the objections others avoid. For Wolpe, the notion that religious ritual is primitive or some form of magical thinking misses the point.

"Ancient can be venerable and cherished," he told me. "Religious practice can't always be explained in a utilitarian fashion. Sometimes, religious practice is its own reward."

Similarly, Wolpe feels that study of Scripture offers its own pleasures at every stage of life that we encounter it. For him, it is not the literal words alone, as much as the experience we garner from studying Scripture that faith adds to our lives. Not unlike a psychiatrist interpreting a dream, we may care less about whether it's true than what we can learn from it.

As to the charge that religion causes violence, Wolpe answers simply that "the feeling of certain groups that they are better or exempt is…an ugly side of human nature. It's not specific to religion."

Without minimizing the deaths caused in the name of religion, Wolpe asks us to consider the historical record that demonstrates that the toll of war has been great or greater in those periods when religion was suppressed. We need only consider the millions of victims of the anti-religious regimes of the 20th century: Hitler, Stalin, Mao and Pol Pot.

Monotheism, Wolpe said, is based on "not how you treat God, but how you treat others"—and in that respect, religion may be seen as a brake on human nature's more evil inclinations.

Faith can also be a salve, or as Simon and Garfunkel put it, "a bridge over troubled waters."

I can report that my daughter no longer asks the same questions she once did. (Now they begin with, "Why can't I?"). Neither do I.

As we get older, we no longer ask so many questions aloud. Our questions become more private: Why? Why are we on this earth? Events occur, and we ask: Why me? Or, why not me? These questions fill us not so much with wonder but attack us in moments of despair.

Wolpe knows these questions well, not only as a rabbi but from personal experience. His wife is a cancer survivor, and Wolpe himself has had neurosurgery for a benign brain tumor, as well as chemotherapy for non-Hodgkins lymphoma, a cancer that remains incurable, but for which he is now in remission. Wolpe told me that it was on the day he finished chemotherapy that he decided to write *Why Faith Matters.*

In *Why Faith Matters* he does not suggest that faith can provide specific answers to our existential questions, so much as that it offers ways for us to look at those questions and the universe differently—and that doing so provides each of us with ways to address those questions.

While writing this article, I happened to have lunch with two friends who both have been diagnosed with cancer, one of whom is still undergoing treatment. When I asked them whether their cancer experiences had impacted their faith, both said it had, but in ways they would not have predicted.

Neither said it made them more observant, but both remarked on how much they appreciated the hospital visits or phone calls they received from their clergy and fellow congregants, and how moved they were upon hearing that others were praying for them. They felt that those aspects of faith helped them endure. Those are elements of faith that don't get mentioned enough.

Religion for Wolpe "is a complex of things, rather than an abstract set of beliefs." What Wolpe feels is lost in the discussion of religion by "the new atheists" is the positive benefits of religion, such as community, a sense of social responsibility, a commitment to charity and charitable acts and of believing that there is something larger than oneself, having boundaries, submitting to a "higher power."

By contrast, faith, Wolpe said, can also make a "disturbance" of life, making life more difficult. As Wolpe put it, the sense that you are put on this earth for a reason carries with it responsibilities and challenges to meet a higher standard. Speaking with Wolpe, you get a sense that this is particularly true for him; that he is a person who is always pushing himself.

In honor of Wolpe's fiftieth birthday, Sinai Temple is hosting a dinner on September 21, at which time he will formally announce the creation of an Israel Center at the temple.

He is creating what he believes to be the first independent center in the United States to promote Israel. Recognizing that a connection to Israel enhances one's Jewish identity, Wolpe wants to deepen that relationship. He wants families to travel there, to offer specialized tours tailored to specific interests, to be able to teach about Israel better, not only in terms of its history, but also its culture, to invite Israeli artists, writers and performers. He envisions perhaps even having a program for an Israeli artist in residence.

"I'm very excited about the possibility" Wolpe said, adding that he hoped that the center would be offering its first programs a year from now, "if not before."

The center is still in its formative stage. Eventually, Wolpe hopes to hire a full-time director for the Israel Center and determine a place for the center to be housed (whether in the synagogue or elsewhere). Wolpe believes that the community has shown great support for Israel and is ready to sustain a dedicated independent Israel Center. A center that, Wolpe asserts, "is not political." He wants each congregant to find their own connection to Israel—whatever their political and personal interests.

Similarly, in *Why Faith Matters,* Wolpe suggests that faith, religion and religious practice are to be valued—if not for what they offer us then for the benefits they offer our children by learning to look beyond themselves, to be charitable, to treat others as they would like to be treated.

Clearly, you don't need religion to teach these ideals, but these are aspects of religion that rarely receive recognition from its critics. Faith, Wolpe believes, offers us a chance to give our children a way to suffuse their own lives with meaning and better prepare them for the challenges they will encounter.

Recently, I went to see the Coen brothers' comedy, *Burn After Reading,* which I enjoyed very much. However, as I remarked on my blog, someone viewing the film from a purely moral perspective would say that the world the Coens present on screen is a faithless, nihilistic one: The characters curse with abandon. Marital vows mean nothing; adultery is rampant. Crimes are committed without much thought. Life isn't valued; murder isn't so much a crime as an annoyance. People are motivated by narcissism, greed, lust, revenge. People don't so much care about their jobs as care about keeping them. Life has no greater meaning or purpose.

The movie is very entertaining, but it reminded me that Wolpe's point is well taken: Life without the benefits of faith is the poorer for it.

The objective narrative of our lives is mundane and prosaic: We are born; we live; we die. It is the subjective that colors and enriches our experience. We all know the power of music or art, of laughter and love to transport us. Why then, not add faith to the list? And what of the connection between the two?

My freshman year of college, I met a woman who told me, "Al Green is God." Now, whenever the first chords of "Love and Happiness" play on my iPod, I know she was right.

Which brings me back to Wolpe the writer—not the rabbi.

It is also worth noting that *Why Faith Matters* is a book meant to settle the soul of David Wolpe, given that his first impulse when concluding chemotherapy was to write a book.

"I love literature," Wolpe said. "I have always found consolation in words, in both reading them and also writing them and speaking them. One of the really great gifts of being a rabbi is that you are expected to translate your experience into something that other people can understand and benefit from. That forces you to reflect on it and create some kind of mosaic out of the jagged pieces of a life. And that's really a great lesson."

Wolpe elaborated: "A teacher of mine, Simon Greenberg, once said that the best sermons are always delivered to yourself. And I would say that's true of the best books, too. The best books are written to yourself. If you don't write something that means something to you, it's unlikely to touch anyone else."

And so, on the occasion of his fiftieth birthday, Wolpe has given us—and himself—a memorable gift.

September 18, 2008

SPIELBERG DREAMS ANEW

Over the last two weeks, lost amid Wall Street's financial turmoil, came the announcement that Steven Spielberg's DreamWorks was leaving Paramount, having found financing from The Reliance Anil Dhirubhai Ambani Group ("Reliance"), one of India's largest private companies.

What does the fact that no American studio or financier made a better offer say about Spielberg, his dream company and the state of the movie business today?

What does it mean that Spielberg's other founding partners, David Geffen and Jeffrey Katzenberg, are no longer with the company?

We should consider this to be like one of those Hollywood sequels, where a brand name franchise is given a new, albeit different, lease on life. Call it *DreamWorks II: Spielberg Home Alone.*

When I last wrote about DreamWorks in 2005, rumors abounded that it would be selling its movie studio to NBC-Universal. Here's what I wrote: "Regardless of whether the acquisition is consummated, it reflects a sad truth: Steven Spielberg, Jeffrey Katzenberg and David Geffen's dream of creating a modern major studio has failed."

Before I bloviate about the meaning of it all, let's begin by considering the storied history of DreamWorks. Once upon a time, more than a decade ago, the three amigos—Spielberg, Geffen and Katzenberg—sought to create a modern movie studio in Playa Vista (and even looked at locating it in the hangar where Howard Hughes' folly the Spruce Goose resided).

Over the next few years, they abandoned the ambition and expense of creating a state-of-the-art studio lot, and, in quick succession, launched then folded a television department, a record label and a games division to focus on films and animation.

These growing pains were costly, and a decade after their launch, DreamWorks' investors, most notably Paul Allen, asked for some payback. In 2005, the animation unit spun off and went public, with Katzenberg at the helm. Then DreamWorks decided to sell its film unit, too.

A deal with Universal seemed the likely choice, given Spielberg's long relationship there (he continued to maintain his production offices there). But when Universal's financial people tried to drive a bargain, DreamWorks' partners found another buyer in Paramount. For Brad Grey, who had recently taken the reins there, this seemed a coup. To further spite Universal, DreamWorks poached Stacey Snider, Universal's former chair. It all seemed very smart. Sharp, shrewd, killer dealmakers—just some of the words that came to mind at the time.

Fiasco and disaster should also have been on that list. The honeymoon was short-lived. Sumner Redstone, Viacom's majority shareholder, a man who does not easily give up what he believes is his (just ask his children), found himself at odds with Geffen, a man who is often paid very handsomely to give up what is his. It seems DreamWorks thought itself an independent studio serviced by Paramount, while Redstone thought he owned the studio. Although in public they fought and made up, in the end one could say they agreed to disagree.

When DreamWorks sold to Paramount, the deal also included its film library, which Paramount in turn sold to investors. By contrast, when DreamWorks sold to Reliance, Paramount announced that DreamWorks was free to take its executives and producer deals, but Paramount would hold on to an estimated 200 projects developed on its watch. What's more, Geffen announced he would not be part of the new enterprise. Snider became Spielberg's sole partner, even as Spielberg also remains free to direct projects at other studios, as has always been his deal.

Update:

According to reports in the *New York Times* and *Variety*, the Dreamworks executives and Paramount spent the first weekend in October finalizing the details of their separation.

There are still 200 Dreamworks projects developed while at Paramount; reports indicated fifteen to twenty will go with Dreamworks, fifteen to twenty are projects they will continue to work on jointly, and the rest will remain at Paramount with no Dreamworks participation.

Executives from both sides declined to say which projects fall into which categories.

The new DreamWorks faces a very changed movie environment. We are at a moment when it is less risky to make a $200 million movie than it is to make a $10 million one (and the return is potentially greater); when indie dramas—well-meaning, well-made, well-acted serious dramas—fail because no one goes to see them, and when no one wants to see movies with subtitles.

The studios, for the most part, have become marketing machines for films that fall into recognizable categories: comic books, sequels, graphic novels, mid-priced comedies, broad family movies, animation and the occasional romance and/or romantic comedy (all with high-concept, easily marketable hooks).

For me, and many of my fellow producers, the business has become much more difficult. In 1997, when I was an executive at a production company on the Universal lot, there were more than 350 production deals at studios. Today there are fewer than 174 deals (and there will be even fewer than that when DreamWorks thins out their ranks).

I can't tell you that the movies produced then are better than what is on screen today. But they certainly are not worse. The net effect is that for many producers and executives, a whole middle swath of the film business is gone.

At the same time, the barrier to entry for independent (non-studio financed) movie making has become ridiculously low—and the unexpected result is not that more good movies are being made, but that so many, many, many movies are being made—thousands and thousands submitted to film festivals—that there is a glut, and many movies, even good ones, go unreleased. In this era, the big studio film is more powerful than ever.

Which tells you something about this new incarnation of DreamWorks.

The new DreamWorks will, I'm guessing, remain among the upper-tier of producing entities. It will attract talent because of Speilberg and Snider, and because it can write checks. But should Snider fail in some way, or should the relationship with Reliance sour, Spielberg can continue to be, well, Spielberg. That is the point.

I did wonder for a moment why Spielberg even bothered to continue on with DreamWorks without his original partners. My best guess is that having his own studio allows him the best way to be creative with the least interference in a multiplicity of ways, to support and mentor others and to exercise his proven money-making talent for developing commercial ideas and properties. It's the best of all worlds: He is an owner who has delegated management, leaving him free to pursue his own projects.

If DreamWorks has not become a well-defined brand in the marketplace, Spielberg remains one. If the new DreamWorks is no more than a supersized production company of a supersized talent, financed by a global powerhouse in India that is seeking Hollywood cred, so be it. So we will stay tuned for this sequel.

DreamWorks stands a long way from what its name once implied—a place to reinvent the creative model in the movie business. DreamWorks no longer represents the dream of what Hollywood could be, it's just another example of what Hollywood has become.

October 1, 2008

CANTOR SAYS SHOWTIME!

At the dawn of Hollywood talkies, *The Jazz Singer* told the story of a young Jewish man's conflict between a career in the entertainment industry and being a cantor. The sacred and the profane seemed two poles whose opposing magnetic draws tore the protagonist apart. But that was 1927.

Today, more than ninety years later, I only had to drive to Westwood to meet Gary Levine, who has his feet planted comfortably in both worlds. During the week Levine is executive vice president of original programming for Showtime Networks, in charge of such edgy series as *Dexter, Weeds, The L Word,* and *Californication.* On the weekends, he is the cantor at Ahavat Torah, a small congregation in Brentwood. This is the story of how these two worlds not only coexist but flourish in one soul.

Levine grew up in Brooklyn, NY. His family was not particularly observant, but Levine attended a conservative synagogue in Flushing, Queens, whose rabbi, Aaron Pearl, engaged him with his provocative and often political oratory—so much so that he continued to attend services regularly beyond his bar mitzvah.

"It was like listening to *Meet The Press,* Levine recalled.

But the congregation itself wanted a rabbi who was comforting, not controversial. So they fired Rabbi Pearl, and, Levine said, "my temple time came to an end."

Levine sang in chorus in high school, but it was as a student at the State University at Binghamton (now Binghamton University) that he first took voice lessons. David Clatworthy, a New York City Opera baritone, had just joined the faculty, and over the next six years, under his tutelage, Levine, who had never really listened to opera before, became a trained opera singer.

"It just opened up this door for me." Levine said.

However, upon completing a master's degree from Binghamton in 1976, Levine went to work not in the world of opera, but of nonprofit theater: "That was the end of my singing."

Over the next decade, Levine worked as a producer and as the manager of a number of theater companies, including the Roundabout Theater Company in Manhattan and The Puerto Rican Traveling Theater, culminating in a five-year run as managing director of the prestigious Williamstown Theatre Festival.

Nonetheless, by 1985, Levine found the not-for-profit world overly small.

"I needed to move on to the next thing," Levine said. "I needed to make a midcourse correction." So, in the immortal words of Horace Greeley, he decided to "Go West."

Barbara Corday, then president of Columbia Pictures Television, offered Levine an apprenticeship. After a few months, the position of director of current programs became available, and Levine was asked to fill it. From there, he rose to become a vice president, in charge of a mix of shows both in comedy and drama.

“It was a great way to learn the business,” Levine said. “Things just progressed from there.”

Levine is being modest: Over the next decade, he ran drama development at ABC, at a time when the network still had *China Beach* and *Thirtysomething* on the air, and he developed such shows as *Twin Peaks, Life Goes On* and *NYPD Blue*. From there, he went on to become president of Witt-Thomas Productions, one of the most successful producers of comedies, a hands-on experience where he was “on the stage every day.” Witt-Thomas led to a position at Warner Brothers Television in charge of all development—both comedy and drama. Among the shows that were created under his tenure, Levine takes special pride in *The West Wing*. Levine’s rise in Hollywood was as well-rounded as it was meteoric.

Then Levine’s boss at Warner Brothers was fired. This was not good for Levine. And given that this coincided with the first internet boom, in the late 1990s, Levine moved to Icebox, an internet start-up, founded by TV writers Howard Gordon, Rob LaZebnik and John Collier, that promised to be the next generation of entertainment studios.

Levine found himself working in a cool warehouse space in Culver City, meeting “with unbelievable creators,” such as Larry David and “almost every executive producer of *The Simpsons*.’ However, he admits, “There was no business plan to support it.” (Just to show how crazy Icebox was, they once bought a pitch from me and my much more talented partner on the project, Sandy Frank, which is how I first met Levine.)

Whether my pitch was the moment that Levine realized that the Internet bubble was going to burst was a question I did not raise in our recent interview, but shortly thereafter Levine leapt at an opportunity to move to Showtime.

Levine's mandate was to put Showtime on the map with series, while at the same time also overseeing their movies and miniseries. That was seven and a half years ago, and "slowly but surely," he said, they've been doing just that.

But there's a whole other Gary Levine story, too. Take a step back, to 1994, when Levine was asked to coffee to meet a young rabbi, Mordecai Finley, who was leaving Stephen S. Wise Temple to start his own congregation, Ohr HaTorah.

"I really liked what he had to say," Levine recalled.

Soon enough, Levine found himself attending services for the first time since high school, while his children attended religious school. "Mordecai does ignite people," he said.

One day, Meirav Finley, the rabbi's wife and partner in the administration of Ohr HaTorah congregation, announced that the shul's cantorial soloist was leaving. Rather than replace her, the plan was to invite congregants to help lead services.

"I was not happy about it," Levine said.

Eventually, Meirav approached Levine saying, "I need you to volunteer."

Levine was reluctant. In what he described as "typical Finley fashion," she said, "That's why you have to do it. We don't want someone who wants to perform." Levine agreed on two conditions: One, that he could in fact learn how to do it; and two, that doing so should not rob him of the enjoyment of attending services.

The following week, Meirav announced to the congregation that Levine would be leading High Holy Day services—just five months away. Levine wasn't sure he could do it, but he and Meirav worked together.

"She was an excellent teacher," he said.

Not only was he able to chant the services, but he said that doing so became "if anything, a deeper experience."

Using his voice to help carry a congregation along was "enormously satisfying." In some mysterious way, Levine's early voice training and temple attendance, all of which he had forsaken, had come together for some greater purpose.

For the next eight or nine years, Levine served as one of the congregation's volunteer cantors. He assisted Rabbi Finley at services, at weddings, bar mitzvahs and funerals. Once, when Finley was asked to officiate at a Wexner Heritage Foundation event and was allowed to invite any cantor in the country to assist him, he chose Levine.

However, at a certain point, Levine and Finley reached what Levine refers to as "creative differences"—a euphemism from his showbiz world. Levine stopped officiating and returned to being a congregant. Yet that, in time, proved too frustrating an experience.

"We drifted away," Levine said.

Levine was without a congregation. On occasion, he freelanced, as when a congregation in Montecito whose cantor was on bed rest called him to fill in for the High Holy Days. But he thought his cantorial days were behind him.

Then, in 2002, he heard from a group who wanted to start their own minyan, several of who were former members of Ohr HaTorah. Levine declined, not wanting to be part of a breakaway group.

However, as the group grew and formalized themselves into a congregation of their own—Ahavat Torah—and were joined by Rabbi Miriam Hamrell, Levine accepted the invitation to come in and chant. That was about five years ago, and Levine has been their cantorial soloist ever since.

Levine describes Ahavat Torah as a congregation for the forty-plus crowd (age, not suit size), whose kids are out of religious school—people not forced to find a congregation but seeking one where the prayers are vociferous, and with intense, interesting Torah discussions. They have fashioned their own siddur (prayer book) with the prayers mostly in Hebrew; it's egalitarian; and people dress from casual to traditional. The drash (or sermon) is given by the rabbi once a month, while others come from guest rabbis or congregants. Levine describes it as "very cordial, very inviting, small and warm."

Let me say this loud and clear: Levine invites you all to come by some time and try it.

"People who experience it, find it very seductive," he said.

Levine told me that his two lives overlap very occasionally. One time, two writers he had worked with happened to attend services and couldn't get over how much the cantor "looked just like Gary Levine," never imagining the two could be one and the same person.

On another occasion, Levine was in the middle of a Showtime meeting when his assistant interrupted saying "Dustin Hoffman's on the line."

Hoffman was not calling to pitch Showtime; instead, he was standing on a soundstage and needed Levine to intone the Kaddish for a movie he was mixing (Levine has officiated at Hoffman family events).

Levine has also contributed cantorial content to "The L Word," (not only the show, but also the soundtrack CD), and even appeared onscreen in *Sleeper Cell*, in a scene where a meeting took place at Sinai Temple.

Which brings me back to my original point. What I find so interesting is that Levine finds no conflict between his two professional commitments. Never has he been called to choose between cantorial and professional duty. (A friend of mine once had a job interview with Rupert Murdoch scheduled for Yom Kippur. Ask yourself: Was it a test? Did Murdoch know? What would you do?) Never has the content of his shows posed a conflict, and never has the content of his religious duties colored his development duties. Peaceful coexistence in a two-state solution, if you will.

Although the leap from singing “Sim Shalom” (“Song of Peace”) to giving notes on a script about serial killer Dexter or *Californication’s* debauched writer Hank Moody seems a great one, Levine argues that characters such as Dexter, Hank or even the pot-selling mom on *Weeds* are multidimensional characters “who are tested—very tested” (and in that respect they are not unlike the very flawed, very human characters one encounters in the Torah).

“I’ll stand by the humanity of the work,” Levine said.

What Levine accomplishes weekly, Jolson in *The Jazz Singer* could not. At a time when we all, regardless of race, creed, or political party, hope for change, let’s take this as one reminder of how far we’ve come. Or of what one very talented individual, Gary Levine, can accomplish that we can’t. Take your pick.

October 16, 2008

KANIUK SPEAKS HIS MIND

Israeli novelist Yoram Kaniuk first grabbed my attention in 2006 when he wrote a series of diary entries about life in Tel Aviv during Israel's war with Lebanon.

Kaniuk, who will be appearing at American Jewish University on Sunday as part of the second annual Celebration of Jewish Books, painted a cranky portrait of himself as aged (he was seventy-six then), losing his hearing, limping and living in a Tel Aviv old-age home—a man older than the nation itself. In his characteristic stream-of-consciousness style, he threaded his monologue with the comments of neighbors, people overheard on the street and local TV broadcasters to create a compelling mosaic of how life goes on in Israel even during wartime. And in doing so, he delivered a view from the trees, not the forest.

Here is a paragraph that offers some flavor of who Kaniuk is and his writing style:

"I'm talking to Shlomo Shva about my daughters, trying to dredge up a little sympathy. He knows about that. The harshest criticism of Israel and the Jews has always come from us. The biggest anti-Semites of all are educated Israelis, and my daughters are as fanatical as they are, but sweeter than most. I'm also a Jewish minority in my home because my wife, who has been living in Israel for forty-five years, isn't Jewish, so my daughters aren't either. One of them, who's fighting against the war today and davka (a word you don't have in English!) for the Palestinians, sees herself as a Jew and she feels Jewish, but she isn't religious, so she can't be a Jew in Israel. If she we're in Germany in the 1940s, she'd be sent to the camps because of her Jewishness, but in Israel, she isn't a Christian either because unlike her mother, she wasn't baptized. What a pity. On the Seder night, when we say, 'Pour out your wrath on those who do not know you,' we mean my wife and daughters. When my daughters served in the army, I was afraid they'd desert and come home with guns in their hands and conquer me for the Arabs, and I raised a white flag and surrendered."

Yoram Kaniuk was born in Tel Aviv in 1930. As a young man he witnessed the arrival of Holocaust survivors and refugees, which he would later write about. He also fought in the Battle for Jerusalem during Israel's 1948 War of Independence and was seriously wounded.

In 1952, he moved to New York, where he lived for a decade. While there, Kaniuk worked as a dishwasher at Minton's Jazz Club in Harlem, where he befriended jazz legends Charlie Parker and Billie Holliday. At the time, he thought he might become a painter, but spending time with the jazz greats made him want to make music with words.

Over the years he has published seventeen novels, a memoir, seven collections of short stories, two books of essays and five books for children or young adults. Arnold Band, at UCLA, ranks Kaniuk among Israel's "top 10 novelists."

A handful of Kaniuk's novels have been translated into English and twenty other languages (almost all have been translated into German and most into French and Italian). English-language editions include his first novel, *The Acrophile* (1961, American edition), as well *Confessions of a Good Arab* (published in Hebrew in 1985; American edition 1988), *Adam Resurrected* (Hebrew, 1968; American, 1978), *The Last Jew* (Hebrew, 1982; American, 2006) and the nonfiction *Commander of the Exodus* (Hebrew, 1999; American, 2000). Although his 2003 memoir, *I Did It My Way,* has not been translated into English, a very enjoyable excerpt in English about his time in Harlem in the late 1950s with Bird and Lady Day appeared last year in Zeek (http://www.zeek.net/710fiction/).

Kaniuk's writing is often like an explosion of words, like a stream-of-consciousness jazz riff, but his work circles back on painful incidents, moments of conflict between man and woman, among family, between Jew and Arab. From his first novel, about the murder of innocent Arab men, women and children by Israeli soldiers, Kaniuk's work has often exposed the uglier sides of the Israeli psyche.

Kaniuk often returns to the subject of the conflicts between Israeli and Arabs. In *Confessions of a Good Arab* (Hebrew; 1985; English, 1988) Kaniuk wrote: "He came to the conclusion which we are only beginning to understand today, that there is no hope at all, that the tragedy begins long before the historians can locate it. That the fanaticism was inevitable. That the country was foreign to both nations, which invented national movements which did not stem directly from their histories, but only from their sufferings."

The Last Jew is generally considered Kaniuk's masterpiece. It comes with a blurb from his friend, the late Susan Sontag, that reads: "Of the novelists I have discovered in translation…

the three for whom I have the greatest admiration are Gabriel Garcia Marquez, Peter Handke, and Yoram Kaniuk."

I couldn't finish *The Last Jew*—the book overwhelmed me and gave me a headache, which could well be a sign of its brilliance (I confess to having had similar experiences with other masterpieces), but better readers than I have adjudged it a great work.

One of Kaniuk's most surreal works is *Adam Resurrected,* a film version of which, starring Jeff Goldblum and directed by Paul Schrader, is about to open. *Adam* is a former Berlin circus performer, a clown haunted by his Holocaust experience, living in a mental asylum in Israel, who finds a connection with a child who believes he is a dog. Although I have not seen the film, it was screened at this year's Telluride Film Festival and was hailed as the finest performance of Goldblum's career.

Kaniuk has been hailed as a novelist of Tel Aviv (as opposed to Jerusalem), the secular city that he has imbued with all the surrealism of Israeli existence.

Daphne Meijer, in *Jewish Writers of the 20th Century,* writes "Kaniuk has not become the general public's pet. He is a writer's writer; his novels are complex examples of highly evolved literary craftsmanship, non-linear in structure and full of metaphor. Yet his work is very humorous…in this respect there is a connection between his writing and the works of many masters in the European tradition of the absurd and the surreal."

Currently, Kaniuk also writes a provocative column for Yediot Akronot that can be read in English on ynetnews.com—in recent columns, he has chastised the Orthodox Shas party for caring more about money than about Jerusalem; argued for keeping Prime Minister Ehud Olmert in office (rather than letting Bibi Netanyahu find a way back in); called Yad Vashem a "Disneyland" and said "the Germans don't owe Israel a dime."

At AJU's Celebration of Books, Kaniuk will speak about his life and the process of writing, followed by a book signing.

Consider that modern Hebrew is a relatively new phenomenon, not much more than a century old, and that in Israel's 60 years it has fostered a substantial a body of literature by world-class novelists and poets such as Amos Oz, A. B. Yehoshua, David Grossman and Yehuda Amichai. That Kaniuk stands among their ranks but has yet to become familiar to American audiences speaks, perhaps, to the richness and depth of Israel's literary landscape. This weekend's appearance, therefore, offers an opportunity to correct this and see and hear an Israeli original doing what he does best—speaking his mind.

November 7, 2008

WILD ABOUT DIAMOND

David Wild wants you to know that he is an unabashed Neil Diamond fan. So much so that he has written a book titled, *He Is...I Say: How I Learned to Stop Worrying and Love Neil Diamond* (Da Capo Press) that is less biography, according to Wild, than "tribute album." Being a Diamond fan (dare we call him a Diamond head?) is as much a part of Wild as, well...being Jewish.

Wild grew up in Tenafly, N.J., not even knowing anti-Semitism existed, he said, "because it took a few years before I knew there were non-Jews." It was at Loomis-Chafee prep school that he discovered, as he put it, that "there's no Hank Greenberg in lacrosse."

Early on, Wild developed a passion for music. He was a music critic for his middle school and high school papers, as well at Cornell University's Daily Sun. A college friendship with one of his teachers, Pulitzer Prize-winning novelist William Kennedy, led to a job at *Esquire* magazine. Wild recalls: "I didn't even go to graduation. I went right from my last class with Kennedy...to editing a story by him."

From *Esquire,* Wild proceeded to music mecca *Rolling Stone.* According to Wild, the magazine's cofounder, Jann Wenner, took a liking to his Jewish jokes. Over the years, Wild interviewed many of his heroes, including Diamond and three of the four Beatles. It's hard to beat hanging out with Paul McCartney in Buenos Aires on a South American tour (Wild confided that on another occasion, Linda McCartney pulled him aside and told him to marry the woman he was dating—which he did).

At *Rolling Stone,* Wild rose to music editor and then started to write about TV, where he discovered he could be funnier and "more of a wiseass."

He also started to appear on VH-1 in its *Behind the Music* shows and was asked to produce one about Diamond, which Wild refers to as "the only scandal-free episode of *Behind the Music.*" In the process, Wild discovered an ability to write TV specials (and more specifically to write for others, quickly), therby launching a successful career writing TV specials and awards shows.

On the Internet's IMDB database, Wild has credits for writing 63 shows, including several years of the Grammys, The Teen Music, TV Land and Country Music awards. Among the shows he is proudest of are *The Tribute to Heroes,* following September 11, *Live 8* and, of course, the aforementioned *Behind the Music* Diamond program.

So why Neil Diamond?

Diamond is the New York-native, Jewish singer-songwriter born in 1941, sometimes called "The Jewish Elvis." He was discovered by Ellie Greenwich and Jeff Barry and signed to Atlantic Records' Bang Label, where he recorded "Solitary Man" and "Cherry, Cherry"; wrote hits for the Monkees TV show, including "I'm a Believer" (or "The Shrek" song as my daughter refers to it); and many more hits, including "Holly, Holy," "Sweet Caroline," "Song Sung Blue," "Red, Red Wine," "Cracklin' Rosie" and "Girl, You'll Be a Woman Soon."

He also starred in a hard-to-watch remake of "The Jazz Singer"; has sold more than 125 million records, with thirty-six Top 40 hits; and played thousands of sold-out concerts the world over. Diamond's most recent album, *Home Before Dark,* entered the charts at No. 1 for the first time in his career.

Now, a confession: I am not a Diamond fan. I like many of his songs when I hear them on the radio, but I don't buy his records or attend his concerts.

When I think of Diamond, I think of Al Jolson, known as the world's greatest entertainer and, not coincidentally, the original Jazz Singer. For me, there is something about Diamond that, like Jolson, seems too earnest, too on the nose. A little schmaltzy even. I respect Diamond as a songwriter and acknowledge his appeal as a performer, but he doesn't do it for me.

Wild, of course, has thought long and hard about Diamond and why not everyone shares his fervor. Wild believes that the areas where many detractors find fault are actually Diamond's strengths.

Wild also believes there is a generation that has grown up with irony as part of its cultural DNA, and Diamond is resolutely "unironic." Further, Wild says, "He is the son of a people who owned a store. More than most artists, he's been driven by keeping the customer satisfied." This, too, is not "cool."

Finally, Wild wants to put forward a theory that among some who don't get Diamond's appeal, he suspects another source: "In my heart of hearts, a considerable amount of the people who are skeptical or undervalue him are people who are uncomfortable with their own Judaism."

To which I respond, much as Larry David did in an episode of *Curb Your Enthusiasm*: Jewish? Yes. Self-loathing? Definitely. But Jewish self-loathing? No way.

Still, I get his point.

As Jackie Mason is wont to remind us, "Too Jewish" is an expression used most often by Jews. Perhaps Diamond is the Ralph Lauren of music—a success by everyone's standards, except those who fault him for having been born Ralph Lifshitz.

Wild's paean to Diamond is intended as a "generational apology" from the age of irony to the generation of Jewish men like Wild's father, whom he thinks we tend to undervalue. At the same time, Wild's desire to write his tribute to Diamond was born from a desire to express something about himself.

In the book, Wild writes that he was at prep school when he first worried about admitting his love for Diamond. I pointed out the obvious parallel that coming out as a Diamond fan among his peers is akin to coming out as a Jew among his WASPy prep schoolmates.

"It is so true," Wild said, "If he [Diamond] didn't exist, he would be a wonderful metaphor for being Jewish."

So consider Wild's book-length tribute album to Diamond to be the author's own "Song Sung Blue."

Or, perhaps, his "Song Sung Jew."

November 12, 2008

THE GRAMMY MUSEUM: WHAT WE KEEP

The Elgin Marbles, the Rosetta Stone, the Venus de Milo, Van Gogh's *Starry Night,* Picasso's *Les Demoiselles d'Avignon,* Pete Seeger's banjo, the handwritten lyrics to Grandmaster Flash's *The Message.*

You might wonder what all these cultural artifacts have in common. But as of December 6, they can all be seen in museums—the last two items just went on view at the new Grammy Museum in downtown Los Angeles.

I place them together because they underline the question that came to mind recently when I attended the preview opening of the Grammy Museum: What does it mean to be a museum? Why a music museum? Why in Los Angeles?

I've been thinking about these questions a lot lately, ever since I heard Sharon Waxman speak about her just-published book, *Loot: The Battle over the Stolen Treasures of the Ancient World* (Times Books).

"Loot," as its title suggests, is about museums whose collections contain contested objects, and it explores the ethics as well as the arguments surrounding the acquisition, preservation, ownership and display of such artworks and cultural artifacts. In her talk, Waxman said that one of the questions that interested her during her research was the history and conceptual underpinnings of the great museums. Many of them, including the Louvre and the British Museum, grew out of the Enlightenment. The notion was that a great society needed to collect the artifacts of the cultures that preceded, both to showcase where they had come from and to present itself as the inheritors and current standard-bearer of greatness. A museum defined what was important, what was worth preserving and hoped to educate a society, as well as raise the consciousness and the pride of its citizens by doing so.

In this light, a museum that showcases the history of music makes great sense for a baby-boomer generation as a twenty-firstst century museum set in Los Angeles, California USA.

When we ask ourselves what has been meaningful in our lives and in our culture, and what is it that we wish to share with our children, the answer is: our music (whatever that music may be). There is a soundtrack to our times; history and politics comes alive through our songs, our recordings and the artists who created, performed and produced the music. The challenge the Grammy Museum faces, and in its conception already has more than met, is to find a new language of interactive exhibits, film and sound to tell that story.

There may be no one more qualified to create a music museum than Robert Santelli, the executive director of the Grammy Museum, who previously has worked at both the Rock and Roll Hall of Fame in Cleveland and the Experience Music Project in Seattle.

"Music plays an important part in our history," he told me. "The baby-boom generation grew up with music, and they are now behind this movement to preserve [it]."

Located at the corner of Olympic Boulevard and Figueroa Street downtown, the Grammy Museum is part of the new LA Live Complex that includes the Nokia Theatre, the Conga Room, and a whole assortment of new restaurants, hotels and other entertainment venues.

The museum is a 30,000-square-foot structure that cost $34 million "soup to nuts," Santelli said. The Grammy organization, he explained, had for years talked about a music museum, and earlier considered opening it in New Orleans or Memphis. All that changed when AEG, a leading sports and entertainment presenter that is also the developer of LA Live, got involved and offered a location for the museum in the new complex. AEG is responsible for building the space and for the majority of the fundraising that entailed; it also committed to financially back the museum for the next decade. AEG has also brought on board major corporate sponsors, including American Express.

Santelli was quick to point out, however, that the Grammy Museum operates as an independent nonprofit entity, independent of both the Grammy organization and AEG, and that he had not received even a programming suggestion from either so far.

Santelli predicts that LA Live will be "the hub of pop culture in LA" and hopes the museum will attract 200,000 visitors annually, although he admits that with the current economic downturn, all bets are off.

I wouldn't want to predict who and how many people will actually visit the museum in its first year, but I'm going to say that if you love music, or are interested in the history of American music (any genre of American music), or the process of recording and creating music, you should go there.

Here are some of the highlights: The fourth floor features a giant table-like interactive touch-screen guide to more than 150 genres that the museum has dubbed *Crossroads,* primed to reveal photos, songs and stories about each genre.

There are also four large display pods titled "Enduring Traditions," which combine artifacts, history and videos about pop, folk, sacred, classical music and jazz.

Legendary objects line the walls, including Buddy Rich's drumsticks, Wayne Shorter's handwritten score for "Nefertiti," Jimi Hendrix's handwritten lyrics to "Angel" and Eminem's to "Stan." There are also letters from Buddy Holly (very nice handwriting), Elvis Presley (with some spelling mistakes) and Tupac Shakur (very polite). One case contains Elvis Presley's 1942 Martin guitar, as well as trumpets that belonged to Louis Armstrong, Glenn Miller and Miles Davis, and Sammy Cahn's typewriter.

My favorite quote, from the "Sacred" pod, is Larry Norman's 1972 question: "Why should the devil have all the good music?"

The third floor focuses on the art and technology of creating music. Separate sound booths allow you to experience and learn from interactive videos, in which some of the greatest studio engineers and recording artists show how a recording is mastered. In essence, what's offered is a free education in record production from professionals at the top of their game. There is also a large room with a giant, curved high-definition screen showing a film titled, *The Life of a Recording,* which tells the story of how certain recordings came to be—the current offerings are “Gone, Gone, Gone” by Alison Kraus, Robert Plant and T-Bone Burnett; Larry Klein and Herbie Hancock discussing “The River: The Joni Letters,” and “Jesus Take the Wheel” as recorded by Carrie Underwood.

There is also a history of how music has been recorded—from Thomas Edison’s phonograph to the Graphophone and Gramaphone, from cylinders to disks, from seventy-eight rpms to 45s, 33s and eight-track tapes, to current digital formats. And one wall is devoted to “Record Men,” such as Ahmet Ertegun, Mo Austin and Clive Davis.

The museum’s second floor has a 200-seat auditorium that will be showing a seventeen-minute film titled *The Making of a Grammy Moment*—in this case, Beyoncé and Tina Turner performing “Proud Mary” at the recent fiftieth Anniversary Grammys.

Threaded throughout are the history and highlights of the Grammys, including award winners, backstage and performance footage, as well as exhibits related to the new Latin Grammys and the Grammys’ charities

Finally, the second floor will offer temporary exhibits, the first of which is called, “Songs of Conscience, Songs of Freedom,” a history of music and politics in America, from “Yankee Doodle” to an iPod that belonged to an American soldier serving a tour of duty in Iraq. The installation was curated by Daniel Cavicchi, an associate professor of American studies at the Rhode Island School of Design. Cavicchi’s selection of songs provide an awesome playlist and really make the case for how American songs have shaped our nation’s consciousness.

“It’s about the power of noise…[as] a political act,” Cavicchi said, “in a broader sense it’s about people exercising their rights.”

Cavicchi told me that he was most excited about having tracked down a Civil War-era over-the-shoulder trumpet (which served, as the band marched forward, to project the music backward to the troops behind), a copy of the Wobblies (the International Workers of the World) *Little Red Songbook,* and a battered stop sign from a school bus graffitied to say "Stop Lies," from a 2007 tour of a Muslim punk band—yes, Muslim punk, whose members I might report are today working as journalists in Pakistan.

My own favorites included Joe Hill's handwritten "Last Will," John Philip Sousa's gloves and batons, Grandmaster Flash's turntables, the aforementioned Seeger's banjo, as well as guitars owned by Woody Guthrie, Josh White and Bob Dylan.

And yes, there is also a gift shop, which thus far seems to be mostly of the T-shirt, mug and keychain variety.

What distinguishes the Grammy Museum from other institutions, such as the Rock and Roll Hall of Fame and the Experience Music Project, Santelli explained, is the breadth of musical styles the museum embraces, as well as its mission, which is focused not so much on artifacts as on the inspiration for and process of making music.

The Grammy Museum staff also includes Ken Viste, who was associate director of the Experience Music Project (and worked with Santelli there); Lynne Sheridan, the public program manager, and Melissa Runcie, who is charged with the public education programs.

It will be Runcie's job to work with schools in greater Los Angeles to get those buses a comin' in, as well to develop specific education programs. Which is a good thing, because while I am the sort of music freak who could spend hours in the museum, my elementary-school-aged daughter will stand a better chance of taking in what the museum offers if she's led through it on a school trip. There will also be family programs once a month, on Saturdays, beginning in February.

While Runcie will be working to fill the museum on afternoons, Sheridan's purview extends after museum hours and even beyond its walls. The 200-seat Grammy Sound Stage will feature panel discussions, interviews and a forum for artists to perform and answer questions in an intimate setting. Upcoming programs include *An Evening With Brian Wilson* on Jan. 15 and a talk with Charlie Haden on January 21. In addition, the Nokia Plaza, a 40,000-square-foot, open-air plaza that is fully wired, will be home to series of concerts, including free ones by emerging artists.

Finally, in case your mind is turning toward that special event you've been planning, the Grammy Museum includes a private fifth floor with a rooftop terrace that can be rented, with private access to the museum (did someone say baby-boomer birthday party or rockin' bat mitzvah?).

Music museums are part of a trend to preserve our popular culture. Los Angeles already has a Museum of Television and Radio, and the American Cinematheque in Hollywood, and the Academy of Motion Pictures Arts and Sciences is planning to build a movie museum in Hollywood. In addition to the Rock and Roll Hall of Fame in Cleveland (which is opening a branch in New York), the Country Music Hall of Fame in Nashville and the Experience Music Project in Seattle, individual artists have their own iconic spaces, as well, including Elvis' Graceland, a Liberace museum in Las Vegas and a B.B. King museum in Mississippi. AEG is also financing construction of a British Music Museum in London.

It might seem paradoxical to open a Grammy Museum just as the recording industry is in perilous decline. But that paradox brings us back to the very notion of a museum: How do we as a society, as a culture, preserve what we value. More music, in more varieties, are listened to now than ever before—we live in a culture where the iPod is on shuffle—old and new artists, pop and jazz, classical music and classic rock, spoken word and rap, all simultaneously color our modern life. As popular culture grows wider in spectrum, it also seems to become shallower. Increasingly, it falls to the cultural institutions—such as the Grammy Museum—to organize, collect, narrate and set in context the depth of our heritage. As well as to expand our knowledge.

And until I went to the Grammy Museum, I had no idea there were Muslim punk bands.

December 10, 2008

MAUS THROUGH THE LOOKING GLASS

Art Spiegelman, the cartoonist whose graphic memoir, *Maus,* won a Pulitzer Prize, was in town recently to promote a reissue of *Breakdowns,* a collection of his underground comics work first published in 1978.

As Spiegelman pointed out to me, his name in German means "Mirror Man" (mine means "Pond-wood")—and revisiting "Breakdowns," now subtitled, "Portrait of the Artist as a Young %@&*!" was like finding a letter you'd written thirty years ago. For this new edition, Spiegelman spent two years drawing an introduction in comic book form, a series of vignettes that Spiegelman described as "a demo of how memory works" as well as a prose afterword—an elaborate consideration of the most fundamental of questions—"Who am I? How did I become this way? How did I become an artist and what inspired this work?"

Spiegelman was born in 1949 (in Sweden, of all places). His parents, Polish Holocaust survivors, were making their way to the United States, en route to landing in New York City, where they lived in Washington Heights and Rego Park. As he renders in the new introduction, Spiegelman started drawing early and as a child became besotted with newspaper comics and with Mad Magazine. He published his first cartoons at thirteen in a local newspaper, and by the time he was eighteen, he had landed a summer job working for Topps Chewing Gum (which included cartoons in the gum wrappers) under the legendary Woody Gelman, where he met some of the now-celebrated early comic strip artists, as well as some rising talent, among them Robert "R." Crumb.

Spiegelman attended Harpur College in Binghamton, NY (now part of Binghamton University). It was the sixties! Sex, LSD and combinations of both blew his mind, while trips to San Francisco, the East Village and a Vermont commune put flowers in his hair, or at least in some of his drawings.

Although his parents wanted him to be a dentist, a breakdown (of the mental hospital kind) made clear that was never going to happen. That same year, 1969, Spiegelman's mother committed suicide. In his comic book depiction of her death, Spiegelman dubbed it "the perfect crime," saying that in killing herself she murdered a part of him and at the same time left him "to take the rap."

After his mother's death, Spiegelman returned to Binghamton, where filmmaker Ken Jacobs inspired him to think of himself as an artist. Studying the way early cartoons anthropomorphized animals in one of Jacobs' classes gave Spiegelman his "Eureka!" moment. He decided to create a comic in which the victims would be drawn as mice, and the persecutors as cats. It would be about…race in America! Imagine Ku Klux Kats lynching black mice! It seemed genius—that is until Spiegelman realized he knew, as he put it, "bupkis about being black in America."

Justin Green, one of the cartoonists Spiegelman had befriended in San Francisco, had asked him to contribute a short strip to an underground comic to be called, *Funny Animals.* Spiegelman decided to apply his earlier idea to a different tack—his own life. The three-page cartoon Spiegelman produced in a month's time in 1972 was called *Maus.* It was about a father who tells his young mouse son "bedtime stories" about his time in Mauschwitz. He drew it in a very simple black-and-white direct style, as he called it, "conventional in form, radical in content." Later that same year, Spiegelman would draft a German Expressionist style narrative called, *Prisoner on Hell Planet* about his mother's suicide.

Over the next six years, Spiegelman experimented with a variety of comic book forms, incorporating elements of pulp detective fiction and porno films, referencing everything from the Sunday funnies of the early 1900s to Cubism and riding a "New Wave" in his work that, much like the movies or music of the time, mixed high art with low to find new forms. This was the work collected in the 1978 *Breakdowns,* the title of which is a play on words alluding both to the artistic term break-down, to Spiegelman's own mental anguishes and his breakthrough artwork.

Much like Norman Mailer's *Advertisements for myself, Breakdowns* was meant to make the case for Spiegelman's art. "For me," Spiegelman notes in his new afterword, *Breakdowns* is "a manifesto, a diary, a crumpled suicide note and a still- relevant love letter to a medium I adore."

Spiegelman then decided to expand *Maus* into a book-length work. When people asked him how long it would take to finish *Maus,* he would answer "two or three years," which he now says was "idiotic because I was saying that for years and years."

In 1982, his father died. During our conversation, I suggested that perhaps one of the reasons *Maus* took so long was that Spiegelman couldn't finish it while his father was still alive.

Spiegelman admitted that although he had hoped to finish the work while his father was still alive, his death, "may have made certain things easier." "My relationship with my father improved a lot after he died," Spiegelman explained. "I bristle when people ask if I think of my comics as therapy, but I will say that to act out [Vladek's part] in this, which is what you have to do in order to draw any decent strip…was a kind of gestalt thing to see it from his point of view."

Maus was first published in book form in 1986 (in part to beat out Spielberg's animated movie about a mouse, *An American Tail*), and *Maus II* came out in 1991. *Maus* won the Pulitzer Prize in 1992—requiring a special category since its form was considered so unconventional.

Maus also became a tough act to follow. In a comic strip called *Pop Art* that is part of the new intro to *Breakdowns*, Spiegelman draws himself fleeing from a giant Maus-like mouse monument, saying "No matter how much I run I can't seem to get out of that Mouse's shadow." The success of *Maus*, he now says, was "constricting."

Then came September 11.

For Spiegelman, who lived in lower Manhattan with his family, the event was profoundly affecting. Having spent much of his life living with the specter of his father's cataclysm, he now found that "something one might call history was intersecting with my story in a direct way." (I suggested to Spiegelman that this was like the scene in *Hannah and her Sisters* where Woody Allen plays a hypochondriac who visits his doctor and is shocked to find out that he might indeed be deathly ill).

"One of the things I felt that morning [was]...'Schmuck, you should have done more comics.' I feel it's like what I can do best. Even though it's hard."

Spiegelman started to draw large one-page panels, which a friend who was editor of Germany's *Die Zeit* offered to publish with a "no editing" clause (*The New Yorker,* where he had worked for many years, passed). Over the next year, Spiegelman drew ten pages. Publishers from England, Italy and France carried it—"A coalition of the willing," as Spiegelman called it, and eventually it was published in the United States in The Forward, which had also published *Maus* in serial form. It also came out finally in book form with the title, *In the Shadow of No Towers.*

Keeping his vow to make more comics, Spiegelman has several works forthcoming: He just did a volume for Toon Books (www.toon-books.com), whose editorial director is Francoise Mouly, Spiegelman's wife and frequent collaborator (he's listed on the Web site as "series advisor"). He's also done a collection of three different sketchbooks to be published by McSweeny's, as a well as *Meta Maus,* an update of the 1994 *Maus Voyager* CD-ROM, to be published by Criterion. And he is working on a new comic that, he says, "I refuse to talk about what it would be, because that would sure kill it."

As much as *Maus* owes to the legacy of his father, Vladek, Spiegelman feels equally that "all of my work before that and after that [owes] a lot to the fathers who made the Sunday comics from 1900."

“Maybe that’s the way I am Jewish,” Spiegelman said. “I was lecturing somewhere on Yom Kippur, and I explained that I didn’t observe the High Holy Days, since I haven’t gotten high since about 1980. [However]…in many ways the Jewishness has to do with carrying a history.”

“The irony for me is that I am involved in this Oedipal struggle, and now here I am this patriarch of comics who’s in a kind of Oedipal target position for younger comics, who might think I’m taking up too much oxygen.”

Reflecting on the way comics have changed since he first published *Breakdowns,* Spiegelman said, “When I was growing up, if you went into a bar and told this woman that you drew comic books, it wasn’t a really surefire pick-up line…Now it seems to be as good as saying that I play bass in some punk band.”

The current comics explosion that has birthed Comic-Con and made graphic novels hot literary properties for the movies, is “part of the trifecta that just happened to comics.”

“Now comics can be anything,” Spiegelman said, “that includes a literary or visual arts comic that could find its way into bookstores or museums easily.” Much as that makes Spiegelman happy, it also concerns him.

“I’ve been fretting recently [that] I placed my bet on this when it was an unusual place to be. It seems I’m living in a Phillip K. Dick world—like I willed it into existence somehow. Now, in the last eight years, is when it’s really flourished. Comics can now be a serious medium—as opposed to ephemeral garbage. I’m worrying perhaps that I used up the seriousness quotient for the planet and it ended up being in comics; so now the world of political and social arena has no adults left in it.”

One could say it was as if from *Maus* to now, the Mirror Man and the comics he begat had passed through the looking glass.

December 25, 2008

TOM IS....

Tommywood is...Tom is...on Facebook. Aren't you? If you read this column online and are not on Facebook, you will soon be.

The Facebook wave has now washed over my generation, the "late baby boomers." In the last two months, the number of people in my crowd who have just joined or who joined a while ago but are now suddenly really using the social network is exploding exponentially.

Why? Why now? And what, exactly, is it about Facebook that has become so appealing?

Launched as "thefacebook" in February 2004 in a Harvard dorm room by Mark Zuckerberg, Chris Hughes, Dustin Moskovitz and Eduardo Saverin, the concept originally had a specific college focus: At the time, every freshman entering college received a printed face book of their classmates with a picture and limited info like hometown and high school.

The bright idea was to take this online, adding an intranet communication function, allowing those who signed up to become a friend of anyone else on the network, but only if they accepted your invitation. As universities were now issuing college e-mail addresses only to verified community members, access initially was limited only to those with valid school addresses. Simple enough.

The next month, Facebook expanded to Stanford, Yale and Columbia. By June, the creators opened offices in Palo Alto, with $500,000 in funding. By December 2004, 1 million users had signed up. By May of the following year, the network had expanded to 800 colleges and raised $12.7 million in funding from venture capitalists.

Over the next few years, they expanded into work networks, added new features and applications and became available in many more languages. Today, Facebook claims to have more than 150 million active users.

I first heard about Facebook a few years ago and quickly got the appeal: I still recall spending hours poring over my freshman face book at college, as if it held some clue to my future social life. I understand why college kids would want to be on Facebook and once it took hold why it migrated both to kids in high school and to recent college graduates as a staple of their social lives. But it initially held no interest for me or my peers.

Even a year ago, the notion of someone my age being on Facebook seemed, for lack of a better word, creepy. But that was because it was assumed that if you were on Facebook, you were there to connect with, or "friend" people half your age. Or to spy—should I say oversee?—what your child was up to.

What then proved the tipping point? What changed to get us to take it on for ourselves?

These days, when we talk about change, we're talking about Obama. So perhaps it's not strange that Obama plays some part in this revolution, as well.

Last year, cofounder Hughes took a leave from Facebook to become director of online organizing for the Obama campaign. Hughes' success and the media attention to Obama's use of Facebook was what first made me consider that I needed to check out the social network.

Clearly, I was not alone, because in the months leading up to the election, I began to get more and more invitations to be on Facebook. In September, I was still avoiding, but by late November, three weeks after the election, I joined.

I read a fair amount of journalism about journalism, and the same sources that had noodged me toward blogging now insisted I needed to be on Facebook. The justification that somehow this had a benefit beyond the social also helped push me over the edge.

So it began—I started with a book-jacket type photo and then switched to a poorer quality, more casual off-kilter shot—more "me" and what seems to be favored on the site.

I replied to the accumulated friend requests I had received. Within hours of joining, I received more requests from high school classmates I had not spoken to in thirty years. I wondered how they could be monitoring full-time (turns out Facebook has the technology to do so for you).

I then used my e-mail list to see who else was on Facebook and sent friendship requests to them.

As my number of friends increased, I suffered moments of moral doubt: Should I accept friendship from people I was not friends with or people I knew but didn't really like? Or even those I knew but whom I didn't want to invite into the privacy of my Facebook world? And what about friend requests from people I didn't even know?

What did it mean to request friendship from someone else? Should I be friending only people I knew professionally? Was it inappropriate for me, a married man, to do so to a single woman? How should I feel if someone ignored my request? How many friends is too few? How many too many? Is there such thing as a Facebook slut? (There is, and you know who you are.)

Within days (if not hours), I learned to stop worrying and embrace this world. I came up with my own rules, which are still evolving.

Thus far, I am still skeptical of causes and most group invitations. I don't feel comfortable having my friends' teenage children be friends on my site, and I don't friend people I don't know (a rule I just broke this morning when friended by a performer whose work I know). All of which will probably evolve further, with time.

What I have discovered is that Facebook rewards certain behaviors that would not otherwise be socially acceptable—such as poaching your friends' friends or even trawling for friends among the listed friends of people you yourself don't want to friend. It allows for a certain voyeurism, an ability to search for others and peek at their friends.

On other hand, it also allows you to find people from your past and reconnect with them, to forge casual relations with people you know slightly but have come to feel you now know better. I have reconnected with high school classmates, my childhood skateboarding buddy and fellow classmates from the Radcliffe Publishing Course.

Over the last two months, as Facebook fever has spread throughout my generation, I have noticed that some use Facebook as a place to be found—they never react or contribute but just accept friend requests. Others use it like a holiday card, uploading pictures of their children or pets. For some, it is a promotional device for their cause, for their art, for their next public event.

The "status update" feature of Facebook is often mocked—it allows you to post what you are doing. For some it is a prosaic account of their daily iterations, for others an opportunity to comment on personal and public events, offering what may be food for thought, humorous, or strange or all of the above.

For others it is an evolving art form—a return of the bon mot, the witty saying, the great line—an art form that stretches from the Greek epigrams to the Algonquin Round Table but seems in recent times to have been relegated to New Yorker cartoon captions.

Still the question remains: Why Facebook for our generation? Why now? Why not MySpace or LinkedIn?

I suppose you expect me to say it's because it's Jewish. That in some way, like Nancy Mitford's "U and Non-U" classification for all things, the other social networks are goyish, while Facebook is Jewish in nature, deriving from the traditional Jewish values of community and of the need for a minyan. I agree that this argument may well be a stretch with no foundation in fact, but what I do believe is that Facebook's appeal for our generation is that it is haimish.

For younger users, Facebook's appeal may have more to do with dating and potential hookups, but I find that for most of my friends, although dating may be one of its uses, Facebook is like the iPod of our lives. It allows us to collect people from our lives, and, much like the thousands of songs, most of which we will never listen to on a daily basis, there is great comfort in knowing they are there and accessible.

Finally, and perhaps this is the real reason Facebook resonates so strongly right now with our generation: Facebook offers, quite simply, a way for me to say, "Tom is…."

January 29, 2009

ZAP! POW! BAM!

Look! Up in the sky! It's a bird! It's a plane! It's two Jewish kids from Cleveland!

The fact that Superman, the defender of truth, justice and the American way, as created by Jerry Siegel and Joe Shuster, was not so much from Krypton as, in the words of cartoon artist Jules Feiffer, "from Planet Minsk," is one of the many things to be learned from *Zap! Pow! Bam! The Superhero: The Golden Age of Comic Books, 1938-1950,* which opens at the Skirball Cultural Center this weekend.

The exhibition originated at the William Breman Jewish Heritage Museum in Atlanta and was curated by Jerry Robinson, an artist during the golden age of comic books, who joined the cartooning staff of the Batman comic series as a teenager, creating both Batman's sidekick, Robin (inspired by Robin Hood), and the hero's first supervillain, The Joker.

Robinson, who will speak at the Skirball on March 5, lent the show many artifacts from his own collection, including the artwork from many iconic covers for Superman, Wonder Woman and Batman comics, as well as Robinson's own first concept sketch for The Joker from 1939.

Zap! Pow! Bam! sets these comics "in context and celebrates the Jewish artists who shaped the values of an entire generation," according to Erin Clancey, Skirball associate curator. The show includes an impressive collection of original artwork, including early Superman sketches, as well as artwork for Wonder Woman, Captain Marvel and Captain America, among many others.

It also offers facsimiles of the original Superman, Batman and Wonder Woman comic books; a minitheater where 1940s movie serials, such as *Superman vs. The Atom,* play on a continuous loop; a vintage Batmobile ride for children under seven; as well costumes for kids to try on, instructions on how to draw superheroes and even a phone booth that rings with calls for Superman's help.

There are issues of both iconic and little-known heroes (The Green Lama for example). And as for the Kryptonite—I can't tell you what happens when you walk by, all I can say is watch out. Kudos go to the Skirball for managing to display so much in one of their smaller galleries.

Also, exclusively at the Skirball is an adjunct exhibition titled, *Lights, Camera, Action: Comic Book Heroes of Film and Television,* curated by Clancey, which makes the connection to Hollywood, including some of the earliest film and animated versions of Superman, Captain Marvel, Captain America and Wonder Woman. Original posters and costumes are included, among them ones worn by George Reeves as Superman, Michael Keaton as Batman and Warren Beatty as Dick Tracy. Also on view is the Batcycle, with its Robin sidecar, from the 1960s TV show.

Visitors will also appreciate the special items in the gift shop, which include not only super-hero themed books and

DVDs but an assortment of T-shirts, capes, superhero-themed kitchen magnets, bobble heads, trading cards, Band-Aids and even Superman-themed kippahs and mezuzahs.

Zap! Pow! Bam! is particularly well curated to make the point that for a brief span of time, a small group of Jewish Americans dominated the nascent industry. Similar to the early days of the movie industry, they were for the most part children of immigrants, eager to assimilate but lacking the entrée into the higher reaches of design or literature. In the comics, they found a tremendously powerful medium for self-expression, through which they were able to both change and influence American culture.

Bios of artists, writers and editors from the golden age of comics are on view, including Superman creators Shuster and Siegel, Batman's Bob Kane (born Kahn) and Bill Finger, the multitalented Robinson, Jack Kirby (originally Jacob Kurtzberg), Mort Meskin, Emanuel (Mac) Raboy, longtime editors Mort Weisinger and Jules Schwartz, as well as Stan Lee (born Lieber), the former president and chairman of Marvel Comics, who would come to embody comics in the 1960s and beyond.

What is striking is that most of these men were from New York, all were young (seventeen to twenty-four) when the got involved in the medium, and they all were Jewish. Much has been made of the similarities between the stories of Moses and Superman, or how, like Samson, Superman has a secret vulnerability (Kryptonite).

However, unlike almost all the other superheroes, Superman is the character's true identity, while the human Clark Kent, is his alter-ego, and Superman is less powerful in his costume of assimilation. Above all else in these stories, readers have always responded to the fantasy that whatever our shortcomings, our true identity as a superhero is hidden inside us, waiting to be revealed.

The exhibition also makes a convincing case that popular comic books influenced American attitudes about World War II and that it was these Jewish writers and artists who helped cast fighting the Nazis in simple terms as a battle between good and evil.

In the late 1930s, at a time when American icons like Charles Lindbergh and William Randolph Hearst—let alone President Franklin Delano Roosevelt—were counseling America to stay out of the war, comic book heroes, such as Captain America, already were battling Hitler. In one volume on display at the Skirball, Hitler refers to Superman as "swine," and Superman refers to himself as a "non-Aryan." Another asks, "What if Superman ended the war?" and has Superman taking Hitler and Mussolini by force before the League of Nations to stand trial.

The comics also supported those already fighting. For example, Robinson created a hero called London to dramatize the heroism of the English during the Battle of Britain.

Once America entered the war, comics continued their propaganda function. It is estimated that comic books were 80 percent of what American servicemen were reading.

The battles against Hitler, Mussolini and Hirohito gave a focus, a mission to many of the comics' heroes. Some fought their way across France and into Germany. And although the existence of Nazi extermination camps took a while to make it into print, concentration camps appeared in a 1942 volume on display at the Skirball.

During World War II, sales soared. By 1944, according to Robinson's catalog essay, combined sales of comics reached 20 million a month. Yet after the war, they seemed to lose steam.

After the bombing of Hiroshima and Nagasaki, they tried to embrace the atomic age, and atomic energy was portrayed as a superforce for both good and evil, with heroes and villains alike having atomic powers.

The comics continued, but society as a whole became less interested. By the 1950s, comics came to be characterized as corruptors of youth, and they began to be regulated for the first time. The golden age was over.

My own golden age of comics was in the late 1960s and again in the early 1980s, as I was reminded recently when I opened a battered box containing my childhood collection that had been sitting in storage for many years. There were the legion of superheroes—the Fantastic Four, X-Men, Sgt. Rock and the Silver Surfer.

Re-reading them, I was struck by, first of all, how well they were written. They seemed more complex in terms of story, as well as their political allegories, than I remembered and much more complex than the movie versions that have become staples of studio summer entertainment. Still, in one way or another, they were all about war and imminent destruction.

In the forward to the exhibition's catalog, Jane D. Leavey, executive director of the Breman Museum, makes the point that superheroes took on the role of tikkun olam, repairing the world, between 1938 and 1950, giving Americans the sense that even ordinary people could be heroes. This was both an appealing and urgent message for a society already deep in an era of economic depression and now facing a foreign war.

As the catalog's prologue states: "During the long depression that followed the Crash, the American people craved not only humor to lift their mood, but also strong men, Super Heroes, to correct their world."

Given that, the appearance of *Zap! Pow! Bam!* could not be better timed. Is it a coincidence that in *Amazing Spi-*

der-Man No. 583, released January 14, Barack Obama gave Spidey a fist-bump?

The golden age of comics may be long over, but this exhibition offers a great reminder of the role that storytellers and artists can play in our culture, as well as how it is times like these that call upon ordinary people to be heroes.

February 18, 2009

HOLOCAUST MOVIES: WINNERS & LOSERS

Are Holocaust movies good for the Jews? Or even, for that matter, for society at large?

This year's offerings include *Defiance,* a story of a group of Jews who were heroic resistance fighters; *The Reader,* a story of post-war revelation about a Nazi woman who beds down with a German boy; *Good,* about the moral compromises of a German university professor in the Nazi era; *Adam Resurrected,* based on Yoram Kaniuk's novel about a demented Holocaust survivor living in Israel; *Valkyrie,* about the Nazi plot to murder Hitler; and *The Boy in the Striped Pajamas,* about the friendship between a German officer's son and a Jewish child in a concentration camp. The lineup even includes a horror movie, *The Unborn,* which features a Mengele-Auschwitz plot point. And then there's Roberta Grossman's documentary, *Blessed Is the Match,* about Hannah Senesh, which was on the early lists as an Oscar contender.

These Holocaust-related movies so crowded the end-of-year releases that at one point it seemed that on any given weekend you had to choose which Holocaust movie to see. However, come award season, with the exception of *The Reader,* most of them have faded—not only commercially, but also in terms of critical accolades and award nominations.

Why? Theories abound.

One issue is the quality of the films: For any movie to garner Oscar acclaim, it needs to transcend its subject matter by virtue of the pedigree of the filmmakers involved, as well as the acting, and it must feel triumphant; it needs to become a "must-see movie," as did *Schindler's List* and *The Pianist.* Among this year's Holocaust-related offerings, only *The Reader* seems to have risen to both those challenges.

But right now, there's also the anxiety of the economy, and audiences today are eager for stories of hope—whether in the candidates we elect for public office, the heroism of a pilot safely landing a plane in the Hudson River, a movie about a mall cop saving the day or, as concerns this year's Oscars, a movie about an eighteen-year-old boy from the slums of Mumbai whose quest to be reunited with the girl he loves involves becoming a quiz show millionaire.

So, more Holocaust movies but fewer awards. So, will this year's bountiful crop mean fewer Holocaust movies in the future? And if so, is that a bad thing?

In my travels in Hollywood, I have always heard how hard it is to make a film about the Holocaust. Some of the arguments have to do with cost—period movies are expensive—and there's the matter of accents and foreign languages, not a big favorite among American audiences. Also, it is fair to ask: Who is the audience? Are Holocaust films going to attract teenagers (the largest segment of the viewing population)? Do they contain too much violence for women? Is the subject too sentimental or emotional for men? Will the films only appeal to Jewish audiences? Many Holocaust movies, made even after a great struggle, have not fared well at the box office. One very successful producer who made a Holocaust drama that failed vowed to me, "Never Again!" It was just too much work for so little return, he said. He decided to concentrate on more commercial fare.

Yet despite all this, many movies about the Holocaust era continue to be made, for myriad reasons, but most often because someone—an actor, a director, a financier—is passionate about a story, or because the story has the potential to become an "important" film (and is most often based on a best-selling and/or award-winning, attention-getting book).

I grew up one generation removed from the Holocaust, among survivors, and as a creative person, former movie development executive and still-aspiring film producer, I understand the irresistible pull of the most powerful story of our era. The pull of wanting to tell it, of feeling that there are important stories not yet told or fully understood, that there are still important truths that need to be stated. Everyone who has ever heard a Holocaust survivor speak knows that each story of murder or survival contains more nuance than any film will ever be able to do justice to—and yet each story clamors to be told to the widest audience possible.

My father, Bruce Teicholz, was, in fact, portrayed by name by the actor Ralph Arliss in the 1985 NBC miniseries, *Wallenberg: A Hero's Story,* which starred Richard Chamberlain, and I confess that I rather enjoyed seeing him portrayed this way, as did my father, with whom I watched the show. My father enjoyed the attention, as well as the attention given to Wallenberg.

But herein lies the conflict: Films tell stories, and they can move and educate people and sometimes even change them. But the Holocaust is a reality and not a teaching story or an action adventure. The reasons a film does or does not work and the reasons we find it a credible rendering of some aspect of the Holocaust exist on separate tracks that of necessity must overlap to make a successful film.

And there's the rub. Because good filmmaking is not about historical accuracy; it depends upon fakery and invention.

A movie, even a documentary, generally conforms to what audiences have come to know. A film has a certain length and a certain narrative structure. There are heroes and villains, often played by movie stars. There is conflict; there is drama; there are love stories; and there is often a point to be made. A work that "breaks the rules" still does so in the context of a set of expectations—and that format doesn't by its nature fit the facts of the Holocaust.

For example, *Defiance* is about the Bielski Otriad, Jewish partisans who survived in the Byelorussian forest. It is a story that Edward Zwick, who wrote, directed and produced the film, and whose important historical work includes *Glory*, has wanted to tell for a long time. Clayton Frohman wrote the original script, based on the book by Nehema Tec, more than a decade ago.

Indeed, the story that Jews fought back, that Jews rescued Jews, that Jews served with the Red Army in fighting the Nazis deserves to be known; it demands to be part of our collective knowledge of the Holocaust, and it is all the more remarkable because of how the Bielskis created a society of their own in the forests of Byelorussia and were responsible for rescuing some 1,200 Jewish men, women and children.

The movie conveys these important facts, but it also casts the plot in terms of a conflict between the two older Bielski brothers, Zus and Tuviah, who differed philosophically on whether to fight and kill for revenge, or to resist and behave ethically. The film also tells the story in terms of sibling rivalry, ego and faith, through the brothers' romances and their human weaknesses.

As a result, *Defiance* had moments when I became choked up by the heroic nature of what the partisans faced, but also many more moments when I was too conscious of the movie-making, such as in a *Godfather*-esque sequence that intercut between a Jewish wedding and a murderous attack on a Nazi stronghold. In the end, I felt I was watching a story and not immersing myself in history, and the personal dramas meant to engage me didn't transcend the moviemaking. In the end, the movie is smaller, less important and less interesting than the story it attempts to tell.

The Reader presents a different dilemma. Its story takes place after the Holocaust, and the film uses Holocaust events to pose questions about guilt and shame, and how that damage, too, is part of the Holocaust story. Based on a novel by Bernhard Schlink, the film sets out to create a hall of mirrors in which secrets carry consequences and assumptions are constantly upended. In many ways, we are made to feel that the Holocaust-era events—as terrible as they were—are just one of many insolvable mysteries of human behavior. *The Reader* feels important and provocative in ways that could have garnered award attention—but it is only tangentially a Holocaust drama.

One of these movies, therefore, is about an important chapter of the Holocaust, but does not succeed; the other one succeeds, but is not really about the Holocaust—it only uses the Holocaust as a dialectical tool. Each disappoints in its own way.

Because the generation of Holocaust survivors will soon be gone, there is an urgency to tell these stories, particularly the innumerable personal tales that haven't yet been told. At the same time, perhaps because the distance of time has diminished the number of actual witnesses among us, storytellers in all genres are now feeling more free to use the Holocaust as dramatic material in ways that have as much (if not more) to do with storytelling than accuracy. Moreover, the more we acknowledge that the totality of the Holocaust escapes interpretation, the more irresistible it becomes to explore the questions it poses as compelling drama.

Holocaust movies will always be hard to make, but no doubt there will always be creative artists with a passion to tell the stories that took place during the Holocaust.

Yet movies also get made because a financier, a star, a director, a successful writer (or any combination of those) is convinced that they can make at least some money doing so. And it is a reality that they become successes more often than not, not because a story is of historical impact, but because leads are attractive, or perhaps because the characters they play are flawed or heroic.

There always will be winners and losers among Holocaust films. Some may be memorable and may indeed have a large impact on how history is perceived. Nevertheless, we must also acknowledge that these films, by their very nature, are—like the shadows in Plato's cave—mere projections, personalized recantations or reinventions of an epic series of events.

So, there cannot be a "good" Holocaust film, only a good film about Holocaust-related events.

Still, despite all this, should we be any less proud if one of these films wins an Oscar?

February 19, 2009

GRAUMAN THE SHOWMAN

Hollywood's Gold Standard

Ever wonder how the movie industry went from five-cent nickelodeons in New York to the glamour of Hollywood with red carpet premieres and the highest of artistic aspirations? Or why a certain pagoda-like Hollywood movie theater in whose courtyard rest footprints of actors is one of the most beloved and frequented tourist sites on the planet? Look no further than the story of Sid Grauman, whose birth 130 years ago will be celebrated this Saturday, March 14, by the American Cinémathèque with a special tour and talk at his other landmark, the Egyptian Theatre in Hollywood. The event will be led by volunteer Mark Simon, a Grauman aficionado.

Born Sidney Patrick Grauman in honor of his St. Patrick's day birthday in 1879, Grauman always said, "I owe my tremendous success to the Man Upstairs," adding, "but having a name that got the Jews and the Irish behind me was what cinched things."

His childhood took him from Indiana to Colorado and then to Alaska, where he sold newspapers to miners, panned for gold and opened a live theater (Jack London sold tickets for him, and Grauman's tales of Alaskan hardship reportedly inspired scenes in Chaplin's *The Gold Rush*).

But it was in San Francisco that Grauman found his calling, opening The Unique, featuring vaudeville performers such as Al Jolson, Fatty Arbuckle and Sophie Tucker, as well as movies, including the West Coast premiere of *The Great Train Robbery.*

By 1906, Grauman had three theaters, but they all were destroyed by the San Francisco earthquake. Undaunted, Grauman set up a tent purchased from an evangelist on the site of the former Unique, with a sign that promised in the event of another temblor, there would be "nothing to fall on you but canvas." He sold 10,000 tickets a day.

A decade later, Grauman, by then "a very high-profile movie exhibitor," sold his San Francisco theaters to Adolph Zukor, the Hungarian Jewish immigrant and former furrier who founded Paramount Studios and who agreed to back Grauman's move to Los Angeles.

On Feb. 18, 1918, Grauman opened the 2,300-seat Million Dollar Theater in downtown Los Angeles, with Charlie Chaplin and Douglas Fairbanks in attendance to watch William S. Hart's *The Silent Man* (the theater still stands on Broadway).

To lure people to Hollywood, real estate developer Charles Toberman partnered with Grauman to build a movie palace there (Toberman was also behind the Hollywood Bowl and the Hollywood Roosevelt Hotel). Grauman seized upon King Tut mania for the design of his 1,800-seat Egyptian Theatre on Hollywood Boulevard.

Grauman staged Hollywood's first movie world premiere at the Egyptian in October 1922 (before then all films opened in New York) for Douglas Fairbanks' *Robin Hood,* arguably the actor's most successful film.

Ever the showman, Grauman gave the Egyptian a rectangular forecourt—perfect for stars to walk between the glow of klieg lights and for fans and photographers to accost them as they walked down a long red carpet to the theater's entrance. The notion of the red carpet, in fact, dates back to ancient Greece and is mentioned in Aeschylus' *Agamemnon* (but of course you knew that!), but Grauman was the one who saw its potential for raising Hollywood's international prominence.

The apotheosis of Grauman's ambitions is just down the street, the Chinese Theatre, a giant pagoda-like building, built at a cost of $2 million and decorated with imported Chinese artifacts. It opened on May 18, 1927, with the world premiere of Cecil B. DeMille's *The King of Kings,* preceded by the *Glories of Scripture,* a staged pre-show with singing and dancing accompanied by a Wurlitzer organ and a 65-piece orchestra. Crowds lining the boulevard for a glimpse of stars caused a riot.

There are several accounts of how Grauman came up with his most famous publicity stunt—of having stars place their foot and handprints in wet concrete. One involves Mary Pickford chasing her dog during the theater's construction (Pickford and Fairbanks were investors in the theater), another has Grauman himself doing so and then asking Pickford to do so as well (the most likely scenario), and the other involves the actress Norma Talmadge accidentally imprinting on the theater's opening night (less likely, since Grauman already had the concept).

One thing's for sure—Grauman knew from the first that his "footprint ceremonies" would be able to drive publicity and draw tourists, long after the theater opened.

Grauman was one of early Hollywood's great personalities. Legendary as a practical jokster, he once sent MGM's Marcus Loew to address an audience at the Ambassador Hotel, only to discover afterward the room was filled with dummies borrowed from the nearby Hollywood Wax Museum. On another occasion, Grauman staged a Chaplin lookalike contest with official judges, with Chaplin himself as a secret contestant (Chaplin lost). One of his jokes almost gave director Ernst Lubitsch a heart attack—but if you want the details of that one, you'll have to attend Simon's tour.

Grauman was also an inveterate gambler. Simon relates a story that as a child, actress June Lockhart was witness to a game where Grauman lost the Chinese Theatre and then insisted the game continue until he had won the theater back.

No matter. In 1929, Grauman lost all his money in the stock market crash. Zukor rescued Grauman, buying his share of the Chinese and hiring him as managing director of the theater and an employee of Fox West Coast Theaters, an arrangement that lasted until Grauman's death in 1950, a few days after he officiated at John Wayne's footprint ceremony.

Looking back at Grauman, his career, and his lasting contribution, it is easy to wonder—who are today's Graumans? Movie premieres are now the province of the studios, and in recent years their event budgets have increased, even as their impact has shrunk. Who today goes to the movies because they saw publicity about a premiere?

Today's movie exhibitors, from Shari Redstone of National Amusements, Inc. to Hamid Hashemi, formerly of Muvico, have struggled to upgrade their movie theaters to make them destinations and entertainment centers, only to face falling revenues that undo their best efforts. Locally, we might visit The Grove and marvel at the crowds, or visit the Arclight and commend Chris Foreman of Pacific Theaters for creating an art theater that can offer perks for a higher-priced ticket. But no one is integral to the movie industry in the way Grauman was.

What Grauman brought to Hollywood remains the gold standard. A Hollywood premiere at the Chinese Theatre, even today, evokes the past glamour of what still remains, nevertheless, America's greatest world export—the moving picture.

But for now, you can go the Egyptian this Saturday for Mark Simon's birthday lecture on Sid Grauman, to pay tribute to the master showman who helped make Hollywood an iconic place for the movies and the world that watches them—and not just by leaving his immortal footprints in the concrete.

March 11, 2009

CITY OF IMAGES

Los Angeles has long held a fascination with the visual; beholden to looks, surfaces and images, it is a city where even the buildings seem to strike a pose. So it might seem surprising that until now, there's never been an institution here devoted to photography. But that all changes this week with the opening of the stunning new Annenberg Space for Photography in Century City.

Located on the site of the former Schubert Theater, in the shadow of the CAA "Death Star" offices at 2000 Century Park East, the Annenberg Space is a freestanding, 10,000-square-foot facility. With free admission and inexpensive validated self-parking, it is a community space, inviting residents and tourists alike to engage with print and digital images. More than anything it is a "Temple of Photography," as Wallis Annenberg herself called it recently, celebrating an art form, but also a means of seeing the world we live in.

Form meets function in the design for the space, by architects DMJM Design: A central exhibition space for digital exhibits—circular in form and with a ceiling that resembles a camera aperture—is surrounded by galleries filled with photographic prints. The floor plan consciously suggests a camera, though at the same time, walking through the print galleries reminds one of a piece of film threading a camera spool. Other references to the medium can be found in the gray metal finishes throughout the museum and floors made from recycled tires that remind one of camera grips.

There's also a full-service kitchen and an area for classes and workshops.

Interviewed at the opening press event, Annenberg explained that her passion for photography is a response to an upbringing surrounded by art, where the focus was always on "the beautiful." Her parents collected Impressionist paintings (which were donated to New York's Metropolitan Museum of Art). Given that she believes "life was far more complex," Annenberg said she was drawn to photography that expresses "the full range of human emotions and gives us insight into our own souls."

That is a pretty fair way of describing the opening exhibition, *L8s Ang3les,* a collection of work from eleven Los Angeles photographers. The show reminds us of the power of photography to show beauty and horror in all its forms and asks us to marvel at how the eye and the instrument can capture a story or encapsulate a whole life in an instant.

Included are the conceptual work of artist John Baldessari, the social reporting/portraiture of Catherine Opie and Lauren Greenfield, architectural photography by Julius Shulman and Tim Street-Porter, celebrity portraits by Douglas Kirkland and Greg Gorman, and the photojournalism of Carolyn Cole, Lawrence Ho, Genaro Molina and Kirk McKoy, all staff photographers at the *Los Angeles Times.*

One wanders from Kirkland's images of Marilyn Monroe, to Greg Gorman's portrait of Leonardo DiCaprio, to Catherine Opie's images of members of the gay, lesbian and transgender community, to Lauren Greenfield's portraits of girls at their quinceañera or a bar mitzvah boy yearning for gifts he imagines will lend him status, or a young girl in the Barney's shoe department. Then there are Coles' searing images of the brutality of war, the reportage of the other staff photographers, which bring our world home to us. What sticks, in the end, is a sense of the humanity captured by these works.

The Annenberg Space, Kirkland told me, represents "the dawning of a new time for photography," adding that he believes the Annenberg will come to equal the renown International Center of Photography, a museum and school in Manhattan .

Greenfield, who grew up in Los Angeles, told me she sees the educational potential of the Annenberg Space in the power of "photography to speak directly to kids." She feels photography is an art form that kids understand intuitively and immediately. What impressed her about the Annenberg was that "everyone will feel welcome. No one will be intimidated."

All the photographers I spoke with stressed that the Annenberg Space's technological breakthrough lies in its ability to display so much of an artist's work at once—a feat accomplished by using digital projection screens and by a series of tabletop touch screens that allow the visitor to examine an artist's work in depth (plans are being made to allow one to order prints from the tabletops, as well). Having a center in Los Angeles where they could see the work of their peers and participate in workshops that will create a greater sense of the photographic community excited them all.

The Annenberg Foundation was established in 1989 by Walter Annenberg, whose father, Moses "Moe" Annenberg, owned the Daily Racing Form and acquired the Philadelphia Inquirer. Walter Annenberg expanded the empire with such publications as TV Guide and Seventeen and was canny enough to sell out at the right time to Rupert Murdoch in 1988 for a reported $3 billion (recently TV Guide magazine changed hands for $1—I kid you not).

Walter Annenberg, who died in 2002, served as Richard Nixon's ambassador to Great Britain, and Leonore, his second wife, studio boss Harry Cohn's niece and chief of protocol for the State Department under Ronald Reagan, died just this month. Wallis, Walter's surviving child, and several of his grandchildren, Lauren Bon, Charles Annenberg Weingarten and Gregory Annenberg Weingarten, serve as trustees of the Annenberg Foundation, which is one of the largest private foundations in the United States and which supports a wide range of charitable activities both in the U.S. and abroad, many of which are the specific passions of its trustees.

Although the name of the Annenberg Foundation is well known to anyone who watches public television, or from their endowments to museums, universities, schools and hospitals across the United States, several local projects dear to Wallis Annenberg are set to open over the next several months: This week's opening of the Space for Photography will be followed this summer by the Annenberg Community Beach House, located in Santa Monica on the site of the former Marion Davies estate, the only public community beach club on Pacific Coast Highway—or as I intend to refer to it, my beach club. And next year, the former Beverly Hills Post Office will be rebooted as The Wallis Annenberg Center for Performing Arts.

If ever we needed to be reminded of the power of art and community to lift our spirits, it is now. The iconic American photographer Edward Steichen once said that "photography is a major force in explaining man to man." The Annenberg Space for Photography gives Los Angeles a place to enjoy the artistry of the surface image and the humanity that lies beneath.

March 25, 2009

JEWBALL

Who knew?

Who knew that basketball has a storied Jewish past, or that a non-sports guy like me would ever read, no less enjoy, a book about baseball umpires, Bruce Weber's *As They See 'Em* (Scribner, 2009)? Maybe it's because Passover is a time of miracles—or is that Chanukah? Or Purim? Or the entire sweep of Jewish history? No matter. We're here to talk sports, a subject I now know a little more about.

Recently, as March Madness made its way into April, I sat down to watch the new documentary, *The First Basket* by David Vyorst—which played at last year's Los Angeles Jewish Film Festival and will be released on DVD June 2—where I learned that the first basket of the modern NBA (then called the Basketball Association of America) was sunk by Ossie Schectman of the New York Knickerbockers (i.e., the Knicks) on Nov. 1, 1946 at Maple Leaf Gardens.

Schechtman's Knicks teammates against the Toronto Huskies included Leo Gottlieb, Stan Stutz, Ralph Kaplowitz, Hank Rosenstein, Sonny Hertzberg and Jake Weber—and they won sixty-eight to sixty-six. That game certainly was one of the high watermarks of Jewball.

Vyorst tells the story of Jews and basketball through a combination of present-day interviews, archival footage and memorabilia narrated by actor-director Peter Riegert, as both the story of the role that Jews have played in basketball, but also how basketball helped make many Jews—for the most part children of immigrants—Americans.

The game of basketball was started in 1891 by James Naismith, a YMCA phys. ed. teacher, as a game that could be played indoors and not take up much space—and it spread quickly through the YMCAs. The turn of the century coincided with the great wave of Jewish immigration from Eastern Europe and the explosion of Jewish life on the Lower East Side of New York. As *The First Basket* explains, basketball became popular in the settlement houses, playgrounds, public schools and other centers of Jewish life. As one former player remarked, "What were we going to do, play polo?"

In the early part of the twentieth century, neighborhoods, labor unions and even department stores had basketball teams. *The First Basket* recalls such now-forgotten semi-pro teams as Brooklyn's Brownsville Dux, the South Philadelphia Hebrew All-Stars and the teams of the City College of New York (CCNY) and Long Island University and how they yielded such Jewish hoop stars as Nat Holman (an early basketball player who as coach guided the CCNY teams to winning the 1950 NCAA and NIT titles); Sammy Kaplan (Dux); Barney "Mighty Mite" Sedran—at five-foot-four, the shortest player in the NBA Hall of Fame; All-American Nat Krinsky; Knicks head coach William "Red" Holzman (the Knicks retired the number 613 in his honor as a tribute to the number of his wins, but many Jews believe it is a sly reference to the number of commandments in the Bible); and Arnold Jacob "Red" Auerbach, a former Second Team All-Brooklyn player better known as the famed Boston Celtics coach celebrated for revolutionizing modern basketball.

Vyorst doesn't shy away from scandals, such as the CCNY point-shaving scandal of the 1950s; nor does he hesitate to mention the anti-Semitism that Hebrew hoopsters met. New York Daily News writer Paul Gallico once opined that basketball was a sport well matched to Jewish abilities for trickery and deceit.

In the 1950s, with the rise of professional sports and the rise of the second- and third-generation Jewish professional class, there was also a parallel decline of Jews in American basketball—at least as players. Many assumed that Danny Schayes, who left the NBA in 1999, was the last of the J-Ballers. However, even as I write this, LA Laker Jordan Farmar is carrying on the tradition (see related story).

As *The First Basket* makes clear, the decline of Jewish players in the United States was not the end of American Jews' influence in the sport of basketball.

Talbot "Tal" Brody is a name that may not be familiar to American audiences. Picked 15th in the 1965 NBA draft by the Baltimore Bullets, he turned his back on the league and moved to Israel in 1966 to join Tel Aviv's Maccabi basketball team. Brody became a national hero in 1977 when he led the Israeli team to a semi-final victory against the much-favored Soviet team CSKA Moskva and announced, "We are on the map, and we are staying on the map, not only in sports but in everything." The phrase has become iconic in Israel and launched a national passion for basketball that exists to this day. Brody's contributions should not be underestimated. In 1979, Brody was the first sportsman to be awarded the Israel prize.

This may seem miraculous, but that's basketball. As I learned from Weber's *As They See 'Em: A Fan's Travels in the Land of Umpires,* baseball is not about miracles—it is about rules.

Loyal Tommywood readers won't be surprised to find that "baseball facts" is one of my weaker *Jeopardy* categories, but even those who know a lot will learn a great deal from Weber's definitive appreciation of the history, the challenges and the importance to baseball of being an umpire.

There is a long tradition of ardent Jewish baseball fans that stretches across the nation from Ebbets Field to the current Dodgers Stadium, and Weber, who I used to know a long time ago (New York in the late 1980s and early nineties), is a *New York Times* reporter who brings both a fan's obsession and a reporter's curiosity to the task of investigating every aspect imaginable about umpiring, including attending umpire school himself and umpiring at games.

Reading *As They See 'Em* gives the reader a deep appreciation of the rules of baseball and the importance of having umpires to define the strike zone and make the calls (even when they call 'em wrong). Weber details with examples from famous and recent games, and from his own observed and personal experience as to what an umpire endures from fans, from players, from management and even from the unions to become and to be an umpire. A lot of it is tough and requires extreme mental fortitude. No one can read this book and come away without a more profound sense of the role of umpires and of their unique place in the game.

My experience of reading Weber's book was not unlike my experience of going to a baseball game: I was excited to begin, and then became anxious about how long the thing would last—doubting I would make it to the end. Then as I settled in, carried along by Weber's narrative focusing on the players, on the game, on the plays, as seen through the prism of the umpire, I suddenly found myself thinking about baseball at a much deeper level.

I now know more than I ever thought I would about the George Brett pine tar incident in 1983, QuesTec, and that at least in professional baseball, the tie does not go to the runner. There are no ties. The umpire calls it.

Who knew?

April 23, 2009

KOZMA'S DESIGNS

Can a piece of furniture convey the story of Hungarian Jewry or reveal the genius of a little-known master? The story of a career undercut by anti-Semitism and cut short by death?

This weekend's "Legends of La Cienega Design Walk" (May 7-9) offers a celebration of design through lectures, panel discussions, book signings, exhibits, guided tours, fashion shows and benefit parties, all taking place along La Cienega Boulevard, on Melrose Place and at the Pacific Design Center.

As part of the weekend's events, Judith Hoffman will offer a lecture on the furniture and design of the late Hungarian master Lajos Kozma on Friday, May 8, at her store, Szalon.

Hoffman is Budapest-born and Los Angeles-raised, and Szalon carries furniture and design from the Austro-Hungarian early twentieth century secessionist period, including the work of some of the most noted from that group, Josef Hoffman (no relation), Adolf Loos and Kozma. I stopped by Szalon on a recent afternoon to hear a preview of Hoffman's lecture on Kozma, an architect and designer Hoffman sees as on par with Frank Lloyd Wright, and whom others have hailed as a "Renaissance man."

Kozma (1884-1948) was born in the provincial village of Kiskorpad and arrived in Budapest at the start of the twentieth century to study architecture at the Budapest Imperial Joseph College, from which he graduated in 1906. He joined a movement of designers called "The Young Ones," who traveled around Hungary and Transylvania studying folk art and local architecture.

Kozma's early graphic design, book covers and illustrations, which Hoffman will show in her lecture, are very much in the art nouveau style, reminiscent of Aubrey Beardsley and recalling Gustav Klimt, as well. Kozma also apprenticed with the famous architect Bela Latja, and worked for Latja's firm. During this period, Kozma became famous for designing the interior of the Roszavolgi bookstore, in which glass panels separated several sections of the shop, which was well known for its heavy, carved wood ornamentation—reminiscent as much of both Biedemeier as well as the Scotsman Charles Rennie Mackintosh and the Glasgow School (although pictures remain, the bookstore was demolished in 1961).

In 1913, Kozma founded the Budapest Workshop, following the Viennese model of the Wiener Werkstatte, with the aim of providing highly functional high design for homes and offices, from the structure of the buildings down to every aspect of the interiors, from furniture to floor coverings and lamps. This all was meant to appeal to Budapest's rising middle class. Kozma's takeoff on baroque-style furniture came to be known as Kozma-baroque and featured what today would be considered postmodern references to Hungarian folk art motifs, mixing luxurious traditional woods and materials in unexpected ways.

At the end of World War I, the Austro-Hungarian Empire came to an end, and after the short reign of the Bela Kun communist government, Hungary became increasingly conservative under the right-wing Horthy government that followed. Kozma, for his part, designed stores including a well-known pharmacy, a department store and a movie theater, as well as a few apartment buildings and even the Kassa Synagogue.

In the 1930s, Kozma designed several villas in the hills of Buda. It was in these homes—where he designed both the structures as well as every element of the inside, from the floor coverings to the fixtures to the type of glass used in the windows—that he did some of his finest work. He partnered with the furniture company Heisler, and at Szalon can be seen a game table with chairs, a desk chair, a bar and a secretary, all of which Kozma designed, as well as his gorgeous club chairs.

Looking at Kozma's work today, Hoffman remarks that it seems postmodernist, as if Kozma had been playing with baroque touches, even including elements of Chinoiserie, as he evolved toward a modernist aesthetic.

However, despite his fame and reputation, Kozma received no public commissions. In his later years, Hoffman said, he claimed that it was his liberal sentiments and support of the Bela Kun government that kept him from getting such work.

More likely, however, Hoffman and other experts believe, Kozma's problem was that he was a Jew in an increasingly anti-Semitic country. By 1938, Hungary's anti-Jewish laws stripped Kozma of his membership in the Chamber of Architects as well as his license to work. Kozma responded by writing a book of his architectural principles, illustrated by his work, "The New House," which was published in Switzerland in 1941.

Once the Nazis invaded Hungary, Kozma went into hiding with false papers. Surviving the war, he was reinstated as an architect, received his first public commission for a school, joined the editorial board of a modernist architecture journal Uj Epiteszet (New Architecture) and was appointed both as a director of the School for Applied Arts and a professor in the School of Architecture at Budapest Technical University. Unfortunately, before the school's new building opened in 1946, Kozma died at age sixty-four.

Hoffman's own story begins shortly before Kozma's death. Hoffman was born in 1941 in Budapest to a very middle-class Jewish family. "My father was a merchant," she told me, "he had a leather supply business." Her mother was a university-educated artist, a graduate of the School of Applied Arts, an achievement all the more remarkable because in the 1930s there was a quota, the Numerus Clausus, that restricted the number of Jews allowed to attend.

In early 1942, three months after Hoffman was born, her father was conscripted as a Jew into a forced labor battalion. His unit was eventually captured by the opposing Russian forces, and despite being Jewish and a natural enemy of the German forces, the Russians made him a prisoner of war.

In 1944 after the Nazis invaded, Hoffman and her mother were forced to move into Budapest's ghetto. "The ghetto was bombed, repeatedly," Hoffman recalled. "And in the winter of 1945, just before it [Budapest] was freed, our building got hit and everyone in it died. I was the only survivor—a three-year-old child."

Her maternal grandparents raised her, along with her uncle and aunt, until 1947, when the Russians finally allowed her father to return to what was now communist-controlled Budapest, where he reunited with the six-year-old daughter he barely knew. He remarried soon after.

Under the communists, Hoffman's father was allowed to resume his leather trade. But based on what he had experienced under the Soviets during the war, he was not optimistic about the future. In 1956, at the time of the Hungarian revolution, Hoffman's father and her uncle hired a truck to drive them to the Austrian border. They walked across to freedom.

Hoffman arrived in Los Angeles with her father and stepmother in 1957. She graduated from Hollywood High School and at nineteen married a fellow Hungarian, who had also fled to Los Angeles. For the next two decades, she worked in accounting and raised her son (who is now married to a Hungarian girl—proving paprika is as thick as blood). But her passion was for design, and in the 1980s she returned to UCLA to pursue a degree in interior design.

In the 1990s, she began to travel more often to Hungary. "I rediscovered Budapest," she said. She also began finding Kozma furniture in former government consignment shops, thrift stores and antique shops. At first Hoffman bought the antiques for herself, then for her clients and finally, five years ago, she opened Szalon.

Hoffman describes the Kozma pieces as "so noble. They were such jewels." She also found that other dealers revere Kozma, as well. As she started collecting the pieces, she found herself learning more and more about Kozma. Whenever someone came to her store and inquired about the pieces, she would launch into a lecture. Doing so evolved into the talk she will give at Szalon on May 8.

In Kozma's story we see both the glory and the tragedy of that exceptional generation of twentieth century Hungarian Jews. The genius of Kozma lies in his ability to mix the traditional and the new, to innovate and create an aesthetic desired by the rising middle class—and yet, because he was a Jew, he found society turned against him. Hoffman, herself the survivor, has championed Kozma, reaching back through history to Hungary itself to rescue him.

In choosing to call her store Szalon, Hoffman refers to a common Hungarian formulation for the spelling of many words, an "s" followed by a "z." I would like to suggest that Szalon is more than that, however, itself a way, perhaps, of seeing the world: Just as the "z" resembles an "s" that has been flipped, Szalon also reflects the way in which Hungarian culture, as evidenced through Kozma's design, bounces between the traditional and the modern, between the seen and the hidden, between Magyar and the European, the Hungarian and the Jewish, and how it can once again bounce between the past and the present, between Budapest and Los Angeles.

May 6, 2009

THE NEXT READ

Among the most daunting questions I'm often confronted with is: "What should I read next?" Recently, I traveled to the depths of the Jacob K. Javits Convention Center in New York for Book Expo 2009, the annual American Bookseller's gathering, where I crisscrossed the convention floor, Indiana Jones-like, to gather publishers' catalogues and advance-reader copies of so many books that when I headed back to Los Angeles, American Airlines threatened to make me check my so-called "carry-on luggage."

"These are books!" I told them—although they responded as they would to a drug dealer trying to make a home use defense. One day, I explained, these may all reside on an e-book reader, but until then, my motto is: Shlep, I must. They let me on.

So, bookwise, what's hot?

As in the movies, brand names rule, and the big books of summer and fall include Dan Brown's *The Lost Symbol* (Doubleday); *The Swan Thieves* (Little Brown) by Elizabeth Kustova of *The Historian* fame; Pat Conroy's *South of Broad* (Doubleday) as well as *Sully,* (William Morrow) the story Capt. Chesley B. Sullenberger III, America's hero pilot.

But what, you might ask, am I most excited about? For summer pleasure I am eager to read Alan Furst's *The Spies of Warsaw* (Random House), just out in paperback, and Elmore Leonard's *Road Dogs* (HarperCollins), just out in hardback.

The fall will bring new novels from Nick Hornby: *Juliet, Naked* (Riverhead), September; Jonathan Lethem: *Chronic City* (Doubleday), October; and Philip Roth: *The Humbling* (Houghton Mifflin), November—by the way, is there anything more humbling than Roth's talent and output?

There's good word on Lauren Grodstein's novel, *A Friend of the Family* (Algonquin), about a father's fall from grace, as well as a C.S. Lewis-style fantasy, *The Magicians* (Viking), August, by Lev Grossman, *TIME's* book critic.

Betsy Carter (whom my wife once worked with) has a new novel, *The Puzzle King* (Algonquin), out in August that sounds right up my alley—a story of two German Jews who escape to New York and fall in love, only to become obsessed with rescuing the families they left behind. But if you are looking for a sure thing, here's a prediction: Mitch Albom will move us all to tears with *Have a Little Faith: The True Story of a Last Request* (Hyperion), September.

One of my favorite publishers, New York Review Books (NYRB), is celebrating its tenth anniversary by continuing to publish books that deserve to be called "classics." Among them, *The Old Man and Me* by *Dud Avocado* author Elaine Dundy—the tale of American ingénue Honey Flood's adventures in London's swinging sixties; Tibor Dery's *Niki: The Story of a Dog;* and Alastair Reid's *Ounce Dice Trice,* illustrated by Ben Shahn.

In November, NYRB will issue Jakov Lind's novella and short stories, *Soul of Wood,* and a new edition of the great Soviet author Vasily Grossman's last novel, *Everything Flows.*

Europa Editions, which I very much admire for its works in translation, has Lia Levi's *The Jewish Husband* set in 1938 fascist Italy, which won the Moravia Prize for fiction. Also of note is Tin House's *Rasskazy*, a collection of "new fiction from a new Russia."

This fall, The Other Press is publishing Miklos Vamos' novel, *The Book of Fathers*, (fodder for yet another Hungarian-flavored Tommywood column), and Aly Gotz's nonfiction account, *Fromms*, which tells the story of how German Jewish entrepreneur Julius Fromm's condom empire fell to the Nazis.

Speaking of kinky, in October, Kinky Friedman will share his tales of celebrities and their pets in a still unnamed book (Simon & Schuster)—his book tour is going to four cities—all of them in Texas.

There are many forthcoming books of note by or about celebrities, including late-night talk-show host Craig Ferguson's *American on Purpose* (HarperCollins); Shel Silverstein, *Silverstein and Me*, by Mary Gold (Ren Hen Press); and, in October, a bio of one of our favorite converts to Judaism, Elizabeth Taylor, by William J. Mann (Houghton Mifflin). At the same time, Susie Essman, of *Curb Your Enthusiasm* fame, has a self-help book, *What Would Susie Say* (Simon & Schuster)—I have a feeling that's some tough love she's offering.

America's favorite Holocaust survivor, Haganah fighter and sexologist offers *Dr. Ruth's Top 10 Secrets to Great Sex* (Wiley), which I haven't read, but here's my own advice for great sex: Put down the book!

Pop Culture quiz: Who hosts two shows, one of which is my daughter's favorite and the other my wife's? That would have to be Tom Bergeron, who hosts both *America's Funniest Home*

Videos and *Dancing With the Stars* and whose book is called, not surprisingly, *I'm Hosting as Fast I Can—Zen and the Art of Staying Sane in Hollywood* (HarperOne).

Another cute volume is Jerry Levitan's *I Met the Walrus* (Collins Design) about how, as a teenager, he interviewed John Lennon and the impact that had on his life, with illustrations and a DVD of his interview (only later did I discover we share a literary agent).

Alyson Books has *My Red Blood,* Alix Dobkin's memoir of growing up communist, of the Greenwich Village folk scene and of recording the first openly lesbian album, *Lavender Jane Loves Women.*

Ang Lee's August film, *Taking Woodstock,* starring Demetri Martin and Emile Hirsch, is based on Elliot Tiber's charming and funny memoir (Square One Publishers) being released in paperback to celebrate the fortieth anniversary of the three-day festival that rocked the world.

If you are hungering for a little nosh, David Sax's *Save the Deli* (McClellan & Stewart) shares his journey into the heart of...well, heartburn. By contrast, if you want to lose your carnivorous appetite, in November, Jonathan Safran Foer will make the case against *Eating Animals* for Little Brown, no doubt in his own illuminating, loud and incredibly close way.

As for serious nonfiction, Daniel Goldhagen returns this fall with *Worse Than War* (Public Affairs), his first book since *Hitler's Willing Executioners,* this one an investigation into political mass murder the world over in modern times. Goldhagen wrote the book in conjunction with a WNET-TV documentary, in which he visits killing fields and speaks with some of the murderers to develop his own theories of what he calls "eliminationism" and postulates what the international community can do to intervene.

If it's politics you are interested in, California Congressman Henry Waxman (D-Los Angeles) issues *The Waxman Report: How Congress Really Works* (Twelve) in July, while Frank Luntz of *The Contract With America* fame lets us know *What Americans Really Want,* (Hyperion), at the end of September.

What do you want in business books: good news or bad? Ace Greenberg tells his version of the fall of Bear Sterns, while Dan Senor and Saul Singer offer *Start Up Nation: The Story of Israel's Economic Miracle* (Twelve).

In the ever-growing world of graphic novels, prize-winning children's author David Small's memoir, *Stitches* (Norton), has been getting a lot of good word of mouth. Judge Sonia Sotomayor will be happy to know Nancy Drew is also available in graphic novel form—issue No. 17 features *Night of the Living Chatchke* (their spelling, not mine).

I can't wait to see *The Book of Genesis* (Norton) as illustrated by R. Crumb, who promises "Nothing left out!"—but if that concept seems not safe for work or for home, you can always hide Crumb behind a copy of The Jewish Publication Society's *JPS Illustrated Children's Bible*—the word of God as retold by Ellen Frankel and illustrated by Avi Katz.

Janet Peer, author of *Yiddish for Dogs,* now offers up *Yiddish for Babies* (Simon & Schuster), to which I can only say vey iz mir. One of our favorite children's dogs, Mo, who last year starred in the scent- enhanced *Mo's Nose* returns with *Mo Smells the Holidays*, by Margaret Hyde and Amanda Giacomini, complete with scent-filled stickers.

Finally, Rebecca Rubin, the newest American Girl Doll and a child of Jewish immigrants, is accompanied by *Meet Rebecca,* which will surely be on many Jewish New Year's lists (if you can hold out that long).

What to read next? You decide. New or old, serious or slight, fiction or non, just follow the dictum of the late Jack Lord and "book 'em."

June 17, 2009

VIDIOTS

If you believe all the tech pundits, the future of home movie watching will be moving to "the cloud." We're already well on the way to where Netflix DVDs will no longer arrive in the mail and sit, unwatched, on an entryway table. Soon all films and many reruns of TV shows will be downloaded and sit on your hard drive—indeed, this option is already available in many cases.

It all sounds great—if you know just what you want to watch—and if what you want actually is available. But the truth is, sometimes I still need a movie maniac, a real person who will steer me to some incredibly wonderful foreign classic or who owns that obscure title I've been searching for. Sometimes, too, I am itching to experience the joy of discovery that comes from browsing real-life shelves at some real-life repository with a highly eccentric collection—and not just computer-generated "recommendations." For that I can't go to the cloud; I need to go to a great video store.

I am referring, of course, not to the usual chain video store (Blockbuster being the most ubiquitous), whose offerings have become more and more limited. I mean those idiosyncratic old-time video stores, like Eddie Brandt's Saturday Matinee in North Hollywood, or CineFile in West LA, or my local in Santa Monica, Vidiots.

All of these stores are suffering this summer, hit hard not only by the downturn in the economy but also by the DVD-by-mail services. So let me sound a note of warning—they will disappear if we don't support them—and once gone, they will surely be missed (like our vanishing independent bookstores, such as the late-and-lamented Dutton's).

Vidiots has been in business on Pico Boulevard since 1985, located a stone's throw from the Santa Monica bowling lanes and across from the Civic Auditorium. Recently, I dropped by for a chat.

Vidiots' owners, Cathy Tauber and Patty Polinger, both in their 50s, first met at age three at the Children's World Nursery School on Robertson. They remained friends over the years, and in the early 1980s, they realized that although both liked their jobs— Tauber was working for Frank Zappa, and Polinger was working in international film distribution at MGM—neither of them was fully satisfied.

"We'd had it. We didn't want to find another job," Tauber said. What they wanted was to start their own business.

They considered several options, but then they read an article in *Esquire* about "these wacky video stores."

The time seemed ripe for a Westside specialty store that would stock videos of the movies they themselves would want to see: independent, foreign and art films. Jerry Harvey's Z Channel already had introduced a lot of Angelenos to foreign films. There were a few revival theaters operating, including the Fox Theater in Venice, and a few specialty video stores had opened, such as Videotheque on Westwood Boulevard—but Santa Monica needed its own neighborhood outpost.

There was another motive, too. Both women were single at the time, and they hoped that if they created just the right kind of store, it might bring in the kind of guys they would want to date.

They leased a space on Pico in 1985 (about half the footage they have today). Initially, they hired a consultant who had been mentioned in that original Esquire article, to help them start their collection. They began with 800 titles (today they have more than 40,000 in stock). They eventually hired a film broker to find hard-to-get releases.

"We would go to these warehouses in the valley and pick among the videos," Polinger recalled.

Among the most sought after then were The Beatles' *Let it Be* and Chet Baker's *Let's Get Lost.* Among the most successful foreign film rentals early on was the Brazilian classic *Black Orpheus.*

Just a couple of weeks after they opened, Vidiots was written up in the *LA Weekly*—and that launched them, along with an event they staged with Kenneth Anger (of *Hollywood Babylon* fame).

Just a year and a half after opening, they expanded, but they never expected it to go on like that forever. They had always been warned it was a "five-year business."

"It always felt temporary," Tauber said. "We never thought we would be here twenty-four years later."

It's been a good run, though: "It was fun to be out there… The customers really educated us."

And the customers turned out readily for events, including ones with film notables Anjelica Huston, Michael Apted,

Callie Khouri, Russ Meyer (who signed women's bras at the event), critic Kenneth Turan and the indie director Henry Jaglom, who has a large, loyal local following. There have also been spoken-word events with film figures such as Viggo Mortensen, and music-scene personalities like Exene Cervenka of X and John Densmore of The Doors.

Over time, different genres and titles have risen then waned, from classic foreign films, to B-movies and cult films, to Hong Kong martial arts films, to anime, films by Lars von Trier and the Dogme 95 Collective, and foreign horror films.

"The store has changed with us," both owners said, acknowledging that their offerings often reflect the evolution of their own tastes. Currently, they have found themselves increasingly interested in documentaries, so that portion of Vidiots' collection has expanded accordingly.

The store's passionate video clerks have also played a great role in Vidiots' history, and have included stand-up comedians, writers and such now-notable cultural figures as Jason Bentley, KCRW's music director and the host of the station's *Morning Becomes Eclectic.*

And although Tauber and Polinger did not meet their respective husbands through the store, Vidiots can take credit for many other romances, not only among customers, but also the staff, some of whom have gone on to marry and have children (sometimes even in that order).

Over the years, Vidiots survived the wave of mom-and-pop video stores that seemed to open on every corner, as well as the rise of the video superstores, such as Blockbuster. Looking back, Polinger thinks that because the offerings at Blockbuster were so mainstream, people turned to Vidiots from all over the city to find titles no longer carried elsewhere. And that's a trend that has only become more pronounced today.

"Kids who are doing musical theater have to come here to find the musicals they are looking for," Polinger said.

Price wars between Blockbuster and Hollywood Video left those companies highly in debt— and devalued the cost of rental to the average consumer. Tauber said that she can sometimes buy a DVD on its day of release at Best Buy for three dollars less than it's being offered by her wholesaler (Best Buy does this promotion as a loss leader)—but what that reveals about the profit margin, or lack thereof, for small video stores is bad news. Vidiots has had to evolve its own rental policies with the times, which include membership plans (for complete details of Vidiots' rental policies, visit vidiots.com).

Business is also suffering from the contraction in the entertainment business here. Much of the shop's bread-and-butter came from production companies doing research. ABC casting had been one of their best clients, but this year they haven't been around much.

Lately, Tauber and Polinger have noticed the store is becoming more of a neighborhood place—with traffic worsening and gas prices somewhat higher, people seem to want to drive less. And the events still can be a draw—a notable recent example being an evening with Oliver Stone.

But more than anything, the store is the sort of place you want to visit and hang out in. Walking around the store is intoxicating—the racks of silent films, musicals, foreign films from all over the globe, TV programs, cult films and row upon row of documentaries remind one of the diversity of creativity in film rarely on display today—on TV, in movie theaters, at the studios or, for that matter, in that approaching cloud.

August 5, 2009

WHAT SURVIVES FROM THE SIXTIES

The summer of 1969 was host to a pair of historic events—the moon landing and the Woodstock festival—that seemed to define the sixties. As we revisit those events this summer, it is fair to ask: What did they mean, what did they accomplish and what parts of the sixties have meaning today?

With the moon landing, there was a sense of America fulfilling the challenge made by President Kennedy at the start of the decade to put a man on the moon—and a sense that the United States had the brainpower, the talent, the technology and the will to do the impossible.

At the same time, Woodstock spoke for a counterculture that rejected the status quo to create a Woodstock Nation of peace, love and flower power, of music and arts—an anti-war, back-to-the-earth, non-materialistic tribe that would feed and care for one another.

A few years ago, I went to a reading Robert Stone did for his memoir of the sixties, *Prime Green* (Ecco, 2007). What Stone said during the Q-and-A, and I am paraphrasing from memory, is that what he missed about the sixties was the tremendous sense of possibility.

It has been argued that the excesses of the 1960s evolved into the narcissism of the following decade, which allowed a culture of self-interest and greed to flourish and dominate in recent times even as the majority culture attempted to repudiate the sixties. That may be true. However, that does not mean that the idealism that inspired both the establishment and counter-culture had no value or impact.

Recently, I read Mark Rudd's *Underground: My Life With SDS and the Weathermen* (William Morrow, 2009). Rudd was the chairman of the Columbia University chapter of Students for a Democratic Society (SDS), who in 1968 led a protest against the university's government and military funding as well as its alleged racism in wanting to build a gym in Harlem that featured separate entrances for local black residents and white university affiliates, after which Rudd was expelled. He became a leader of the radical Weathermen organization, which decided, wrongly he now admits, to embrace armed revolution and to splinter off from student mobilization against the Vietnam War. Following the accidental explosion of a bomb meant for a dance at a military base, which killed several of his comrades in a New York townhouse, Rudd spent the next seven years—the greater part of the 1970s—living "underground," which meant doing construction jobs and watching as an outsider as the anti-war movement succeeded and the Vietnam War ended. He surrendered to authorities in 1978, settling the charges against him for two years probation and a $2,000 fine.

Although my description above makes Rudd seem undistinguished, it is his account of the times, the passions, the mistakes, even the infighting and settling of petty rivalries that make Rudd's book worth reading. (As a side note, Rudd's memoir makes frequent reference to his Jewish background and upbringing as well as those of several fellow radicals.)

Throughout history there have been hinge moments, times when society experienced seismic shifts and convulsions. Certainly one might think of the second half of the eighteenth century with the American and French Revolutions as precedents—a time when citizens held forth embracing revolutionary ideals, and the establishment was toppled.

Yet the revolution in France was followed by the Reign of Terror and then the rule of Napoleon. In our own country, the revolutions of 1969 were followed by the election of Richard Nixon.

Vladimir Ilyich Lenin described the struggle for progress as "one step forward, two steps back." In some ways that summarizes the progress made since the sixties.

A few years ago, Howard Zinn issued *Readings From Voices of a People's History of the United States* (Seven Stories Press, 2006), an audio companion to *The People's History of the United States.* I recommend listening to the segments on the civil rights movement.

It is hard to grasp that little more than forty years ago, policemen set dogs on African Americans protesting to end segregation, and that beatings, lynchings and bombings occurred over the rights of African Americans not only to register to vote, but to attend public school, state colleges and universities, sit at lunch counters, and yes, ride in the front of the bus.

The violence of passions inflamed by the movement against the Vietnam War is also hard to appreciate today.

I remember the day in 1970 when, as a teenager, I heard that National Guardsmen had shot four student protesters on the campus of Kent State University in Ohio. "Now they're shooting students," someone said to me. It felt like we were in a state of war—it was "us" (students/anti-war demonstrators) versus "them" (the government/the "establishment"). Although the protesters were right to fear that the government was spying on them, there was a great deal of paranoia, which only heightened the rancor on both sides, escalating a sense of civil war and provoking violence.

The battles of the sixties were the start of a growing divide, a polarization that grew until it seemed the whole nation had become a patchwork quilt rather than a melting pot, a collection of different interest groups rather than a United States.

Yet that is where the sixties took us, not what inspired them or where they began. The sense of possibility, the resolve to stand up to the status quo caused change. If we compare the beginning of the sixties to today—the battles fought for the civil rights of minorities, women, gays and lesbians—they may not be over, they may not be done, but they certainly have taken many steps forward (even if occasionally it seems like we are taking a step back).

We are again fighting a foreign war, but this time there is no disrespect for the soldiers and this time we elected a president who campaigned against the war.

Which brings me to our current president. Could Obama have even considered being president if not for the sixties? Could we even consider a President Barack Hussein Obama if not for the sixties? There is certainly an echo of the sixties in his idealism and his calls to reject the status quo as well as to heal our nation and the world. Counterculture ideals have morphed into mainstream goals.

Forty years ago this summer, man walked on the moon, and for three days the Woodstock Nation convened to show the world American ideals worth remembering.

August 11, 2009

THE KRAFT OF MOVIE MUSIC

"If there's music in a movie," said Robert Kraft, president of Fox Music, "whether on screen, or underscore, or someone is playing guitar in a scene, I'm involved."

That includes the decisions concerning music at every level: "How it's paid for, is it creatively appropriate to the film, is it legal, is it focused on selling more movie tickets if it can be… basically every musical aspect of a film at Fox is my responsibility," he said.

Kraft is in his fifteenth year at the helm of Fox's music division, longevity that belies his journey from songwriter and performing artist to executive. However, if Kraft has become assured in his professional role, he confided that only recently has he become comfortable in and proud of his Jewish identity.

Kraft grew up in Princeton, NJ. His mother, Eve Kraft, was executive director of the United States Tennis Association, and while he spent summers at the Chase Tennis Center, he stood out at camp for always "being on the piano."

From fifth grade on, he was in bands. Although he attended prep school at Lawrenceville and college at Harvard, his goal upon graduation in 1976 was to move to Manhattan and become a songwriter.

"I had no idea what I was doing," he said in retrospect.

Kraft, a fan of "jazzy bohemian pop" started his band, Robert Kraft and The Ivory Coast, in 1978 and was signed the following year by RSO Records, the label founded by Robert Stigwood and most famous for the Bee Gees and *Saturday Night Fever.* Kraft toured the Northeast, playing Radio City Music Hall, not once, but twice, opening for The Manhattan Transfer and America.

Despite those memorable moments, Kraft was learning "how rocky a career as an artist can be." To wit: Although Kraft's first record was a critical success, his second was never released because RSO collapsed. His third, on RCA Records, released in 1983, Kraft recalled, "tanked immediately."

"Teetering on the edge of being out of work," Kraft received a call from Ken Ehrlich, a TV producer in Los Angeles who wanted to use one of Kraft's songs, "On the Westside," in his show, *Fame.*

At the end of the week, Ehrlich (who today produces the Grammys) asked Kraft if he might write a song for the following week's show. Kraft decided to move to Los Angeles with his wife.

Over the next few years, Kraft's career evolved unpredictably from writing songs for TV shows (including the theme for *Who's the Boss?*) to writing songs for and with performers (including 1984's "Something in Your Heart Has Been Telling Me," which Bette Midler released on her recent compilation album, *Jackpot,* twenty-four years later). Being asked to produce songs for Disney's *The Little Mermaid* led to Kraft producing records and soundtracks.

His first million-selling record came as a result of his friendship with an actor from his bartending days at Café Central in New York, who crashed on Kraft's couch after coming to Los Angeles to audition for the lead on a TV show. That friend: Bruce Willis; the show: *Moonlighting*; the album: *The Return of Bruno.* Kraft produced the album for Motown Records; it sold 1.2 million copies and featured two Top Ten singles, "Respect Yourself" and "Under the Boardwalk."

"It sounds fun in retrospect, but with each [project] I went from the highest of highs to 'I'll never work again,'" he said.

Kraft continued to vary his music gigs. By his late thirties, he had worked for Quincy Jones, been a film composer (something he never felt comfortable doing), and wrote and composed "Beautiful Maria of My Soul," the Oscar-nominated song from "The Mambo Kings," with Arne Glimcher, and had started the Henson Recording Studios for The Jim Henson Company.

One day, out of the blue, Bill Mechanic, then chairman of 20th Century Fox Film division, invited Kraft to lunch and offered him the job of Fox's music chief. Kraft hesitated. Would taking the job mean he was abandoning being an artist? Would he become, in the words of one of his friends, "a suit"?

Kraft's mother suggested he try it for two years. Bruce Willis said, "You know all the other things…try this."

"Who would have known that it would fit me like a glove?" Kraft asked.

Kraft, who has worked on some 300 movies, said, "It took me 10 years to feel reasonably confident.

"There's no end to my appetite for hearing new music," he said. Part of his success, he freely admits, is that he has a young, talented staff whose job is to keep him informed about new music and new composers.

On the other hand, the world of movie composers and musicians is small enough that by now there are few people Kraft hasn't worked with or doesn't have an opinion about. That, too, is part of the job.

"Quincy Jones once told me that the best producer is the one with the best Rolodex," Kraft said. That means knowing the right person to call in any given situation. As an example, Kraft cites calling T-Bone Burnett to ask whether Joaquin Phoenix and Reese Witherspoon could carry the Johnny Cash biopic "Walk the Line" as singers. When Burnett, after spending a week recording the stars in his living room reported, "They are going to kill this," Kraft was able to reassure Fox. "If they'd been horrible, it would have been my ass," Kraft said.

At the same time, over the last few years, Kraft has been on a journey that has made him more at home with his Jewish identity.

Growing up, Kraft was very aware of "the mythic aspect of his forebears" and their reputation as erudite German Jews. His paternal grandmother was Pauline Seligman, part of the wealthy German Jews in New York known as "Our Crowd," as were his mother's family, who were Friedmans of Philadelphia. His parents were introduced through German Jewish relatives, and his father proposed the night they met.

His family celebrated Christmas with a well-decorated tree, and there were chocolate bunnies to be had at Easter. Kraft describes his father's attitude toward Judaism as "very reluctant." What his father valued, Kraft said, was "access," which meant successful assimilation and acceptance in WASP society.

A few summers ago, Kraft's oldest son saw a painting in an Austrian museum by a Jerome Krafft, from 1820, and wondered whether the artist might be a forebear (Krafft was the family name's original spelling). Kraft was intrigued.

Knowing that his father had been born in Wheeling, W. Va., Kraft Googled "Jews in Wheeling, West Virginia." He found a site devoted to a synagogue in Wheeling that featured a Kraft reading room. Kraft "had a complete moment of goose bumps" when he discovered the synagogue's president at the turn of the 20th century was named Samuel Kraft.

The Web site listed a local genealogist, Julian Preisler, whom Kraft hired to research his family history. Over the next year, Preisler unearthed a wealth of information, tracing the family back to Eva Ahrens of Amsterdam, born in 1790, who came to the United States in 1838 as part of a group of Dutch Jews. Kraft also learned that ancestors from both his father's and mother's families, Krafts and Friedmans, may have lived at one time in the same city in Germany.

The Krafts came to Wheeling in the 1860s. Despite being foreigners and despite their desire to assimilate, what the Krafts did in Wheeling was found a synagogue. His great-grandfather, Samuel, raised the money and was a president of the congregation, as was his grandfather, Louis.

"Five generations ago," his forebears, Kraft said, "were proudly and overtly Jewish." This touched Kraft, who was struck by "the bravery of it."

Today, Kraft wonders why his father abandoned this pride in their identity.

Last summer Kraft and his family traveled to Israel, a trip that further reinforced his feelings about being Jewish. "What the last few years have done in a subtle way," Kraft said, is bring him to abandon the last vestiges of his father's attitude of being "careful" about being Jewish.

Kraft now wonders what the next step might be: "Will I get bar mitzvahed?"

He doesn't know. But one thing's for sure—if it happens, there's bound to be great music at the reception.

September 16, 2009

SHADOWS OF THE SUN

When the German forces surrendered to the Allies in May 1945, World War II in Europe ended. However, for the Jewish survivors of the Holocaust, the trauma of what they endured wasn't over. For many, the effects lingered on in ways large and small, noticeable and not, often in ways their families came to know.

Rita Lurie was one such person. She survived the war in hiding, a young child hidden for two years in a Polish farmhouse attic with more than a dozen members of her family, and she witnessed both her mother and her infant brother perish before her eyes. At war's end, she passed through a succession of Displaced Persons camps along with her extended family before arriving in New York. Her father remarried, to a Holocaust survivor he met in the DP camps.

In time, Lurie herself married and moved to California, where she raised three children. Her eldest daughter, Leslie, became quite accomplished: while an undergraduate at UCLA, she held the student seat on the California Board of Regents; after graduating UCLA Law School, she held a 9th Circuit clerkship; she was an NBC television executive and producer; she was a founding board member and past president of the Alliance for Children's Rights; she is a member and former president of the Los Angeles County Board of Education and has been on the board of several other nonprofits. She married Cliff Gilbert, an attorney (they have since hyphenated their names as Gilbert-Lurie), and they are parents to two children and a stepson.

Reading this, you might think that you already know everything you need to know about Rita Lurie and Leslie Gilbert-Lurie—another story of the triumphs of a Holocaust survivor and her overachieving progeny—but in the pair's recently published *Bending Toward the Sun: A Mother and Daughter Memoir* (Harper), the reader is given an extraordinarily candid account of the deep impact the Holocaust has had on survivors and their descendents.

I recently sat down with Lurie and Gilbert-Lurie to discuss how the book evolved and the insights it yielded.

Lurie explained that she was encouraged to write her story because of the feedback she received from students when she spoke at schools. Although she feared her stories would seem frightening, the students found them inspiring. Lurie wanted to record those stories, and she wanted to pay tribute to her mother and the others who had died in the Holocaust.

Over the years, Lurie had written bits and parts of her story for herself. Various friends had encouraged her to write her story more fully and even offered to help her, but Lurie found the process difficult and frustrating. At one point, Gilbert-Lurie offered, "Maybe I could help you write it." Her mother was ready to start immediately.

"I don't think she heard the word 'maybe,'" Gilbert-Lurie now says.

"I really wanted those stories out there," Lurie said. "Frankly, I thought it would be cathartic."

The process took twelve years. The first several were taken up by fact gathering. Two or three times a week, Gilbert-Lurie met with her mother, getting her to tell her story from the beginning. At the same time, they realized they also needed to consult Lurie's sister, two of her uncles and three first cousins, all of whom had also survived in the attic and were still alive. So they traveled to interview them.

Almost from the start, Gilbert-Lurie sensed that she wanted to tell her mother's story, but also how it had impacted her.

"I knew that my mother's story was distinctive," Gilbert-Lurie said. Very few families were able to survive hiding together in such large numbers for so many months, as has been so famously illustrated by Anne Frank's story. At the same time, Gilbert-Lurie was well aware that the world might react with, "Oh, not another Holocaust story."

"We wanted to tell the story a different way," she said. So Lurie tells her story with extraordinary attention to detail, both factual and emotional. "I think I hung onto those facts and details," she said, "because it made me feel more complete. I wasn't just a mannequin; I was a person."

Lurie relates her life after the war and in the United States, and the difficulties she has had in her relationships with her family members, relatives and in feeling loved, as well as the roles her husband and her children have played in her life. She is unusually honest and extremely frank about her feelings of inadequacy and about her years of therapy and episodes of recurring severe depression.

Lurie told me that she surprised even herself with her candor.

She also describes how, after the war, she was molested—once by a survivor in the DP camps and another time by a relative. These events, she says, "had a profound impact on me, and that I worked through in therapy." She was concerned about possible reactions to such revelations, but felt they needed to be in the narrative.

Gilbert-Lurie stressed that the book makes the point that no one is all good or all bad. In Poland, Lurie's family may have been saved because a German told them not to show up at the train deportation. It was Polish peasants who hid them, and there were others who did not denounce them, although their attic hiding place was not a complete secret (the extra body heat melted the snow on the roof—a giveaway). And on the other side, not all the Holocaust's survivors were good people.

The book's second part includes Gilbert-Lurie's account of her life, including her extreme separation anxiety, as well as the separation anxiety that her own daughter, representing the third generation, has experienced. Gilbert-Lurie said that writing about herself was in some ways more difficult than writing her mother's story, in part because she knew it would be less dramatic. Nevertheless, she felt it was important to share how the trauma of one generation impacts the next, and the one after that. Whether the reason for the impact is biological, as some scientists are now suggesting, or psychological or sociological is not as important for Gilbert-Lurie as recording that it occurs.

"There are so many children in so many parts of the world who experience deep trauma and don't get the psychological help they need," Gilbert-Lurie said. "I want people to be aware it's not just their generation...but generations after that will be more fearful and more anxious as a result of what their parents went through, and there are probably ways to mitigate that if we are aware of some of this impact."

Gilbert-Lurie recounts how at one family gathering, one of her relatives said of her fellow survivors, "We're all still half-numb."

Writing the book was difficult, and on occasion the authors had to take breaks from the material. At the same time, Lurie became very attached to the experience of working on the book with her daughter—so much so that after they finished she felt a tremendous loss. And to this day she is plagued by feelings of guilt—often in the face of her own or her children's or grand-children's happiness. Still, Lurie says, "one thing I don't want is pity," adding, "I am very happy with my life. I feel very blessed." To which Gilbert-Lurie is quick to add, "My mother was very focused on giving us the love and security they never had."

Yet…yet there is a private world of deeply felt emotions that *Bending Toward the Sun* exposes, revealing the long shadow of the Holocaust from generation to generation.

October 21, 2009

EXTRAORDINARY ODDITIES

Ricky Jay

Ladies and Gentlemen, are you seeking a spectacle that will amaze, entertain and educate you? An evening in which you will encounter some of the most remarkable figures from the history of entertainment, such as Cinquevalli, *The King of the Jugglers,* or George Anderson, *The Living Skeleton,* or perhaps a learned goose, a sapient pig or a singing mouse?

A night in which the choice will be yours: to spend time with the famous Siamese twins Chang and Eng, or perhaps the less well known but equally well connected Millie-Christine? Then better hurry, hurry to order tickets because for ten nights only (December 29, 2009-January 10, 2010), Ricky Jay is bringing his new show to the Geffen Playhouse, a show titled *A Rogue's Gallery: An Evening of Conversation and Performance.*

Jay will offer up a selection of images from his own collection of memorabilia of astonishing performers, remarkable attractions and visual deceptions, both famous and infamous, little-known and celebrated. Each night the audience will select from among the proffered images, jukebox-like, to set the play list for the evening's entertainment. No two evenings will be alike, and all the material will be new to Los Angeles. This combination of narrative and performance, Jay told me recently, "is the thing that I've always wanted to do."

I've met Jay before. He and I once spent a very companionable week together, visiting the various movie studio lots and executive offices in Hollywood pitching a remake of a 1930s gem of a movie about a family of con artists. Although we never sold that pitch, I came away with a deep appreciation for Jay's love of narrative, his pleasure in polysyllabic complications and orotund phraseology and his encyclopedic knowledge of the habits of obscure dog breeds—a plot point involved a dog, which Jay embroidered in each telling, always changing the breed, at times offering up the antics of a Neapolitan Mastiff, a Portuguese water dog or even a Hungarian vizsla.

Good times, they were...good times. But where was I?

Ah yes, Ricky Jay.

Jay—actor, sleight-of-hand artist, cultural historian and deception consultant—is not overly attached to his personal history. His Web site defers to a 1993 profile by Mark Singer in The New Yorker, which, Jay claims, "tells you more about me than I know myself." Some of the facts gleaned from that lengthy opus and other sources are that Jay was born in Brooklyn, NY, as Richard Jay Potash, and that his maternal grandfather was Max Katz, an accountant who was at one time the president of the Society of American Magicians and who supported Jay in his love of magic and the lore of those who practice it.

At the age of four, Jay performed his first trick for an audience, and he continued to perform throughout his childhood, appearing on occasion on TV. He logged many hours at Flosso's magic shop at 34th Street and 8th Avenue in Manhattan. Jay so loved Flosso, whose given name was Albert Levinson, that at Jay's request, Flosso performed at Jay's bar mitzvah. What's more, when David Goyer recently wrote a role for Jay on his TV program *Flash Forward,* Goyer named the character Flosso (more reference than tribute—it should be noted—as Jay's character was a killer). Flosso remains a touchstone, and Jay confided that he might project some rare video of Flosso as part of *Rogue's Gallery.*

Jay attended many colleges, and although he never matriculated he did graduate to appearing on *The Tonight Show* as well as performing on the bill with various music acts, including Ike and Tina Turner and the Nitty Gritty Dirt Band. In Los Angeles, he performed at McCabe's in Santa Monica and the Magic Castle in Hollywood. His film and TV career is extensive and includes appearing in a James Bond film, as well as several of Paul Thomas Anderson's works, and iconic series such as *The X-Files* and *Deadwood.* He has created and starred in several TV specials and written several books, including *Learned Pigs and Fireproof Women* (Farrar, Straus and Giroux/Noonday Books, 1986), *Cards as Weapons* (Warner Books, 1988) and *Jay's Journal of Anomalies* (Quantuck Lane Press, 2003). He is currently working on another TV project and considering a book based on his KCRW radio pieces.

However, Jay's most fruitful creative relationship may be, in his words, his "wonderful association" with David Mamet. Jay has appeared in many of Mamet's films, and Mamet directed

Jay's celebrated stage shows, *Ricky Jay and His 52 Assistants* and *On the Stem.* When we spoke, Jay said that he values Mamet's thoughts and suggestions "enormously" and values Mamet's acumen, particularly for the new show, which because of its nature—part conversation, part performance—made it more challenging to stage. For *A Rogue's Gallery,* Mamet is credited as *Director of Prison Operations.*

At the time of Singer's New Yorker profile, Jay was the curator of the Mulholland Library of Conjuring and the Allied Arts—a collection of magician-related tomes, artifacts and ephemera—his tenure ended with the owner's bankruptcy (not caused by Jay) and the auction of the collection (which was acquired by David Copperfield).

"One of the strangest things about that whole episode," Jay said of the sale, "is that it resurrected my performing career." It also caused him to start collecting again.

In 2007, the Hammer Museum organized a show called *Extraordinary Exhibitions: Broadsides From the Ricky Jay Collection,* a selection of more than eigthy handbills from the seventeenth, eighteenth and nineteenth centuries that advertise a mix of what the catalogue referred to as "sensational, scientific, satisfying, silly and startling attractions" also featured in Jay's book *Extraordinary Exhibitions* (Quantuck Lane, 2005).

That exhibition, in part, inspired the upcoming Geffen performances—"seeing it so wonderfully mounted made me wonder if there was some way to actually use this in a theatrical manner," Jay said.

Beyond his scholarship, what distinguishes Jay's performances is their narrative, literary quality. Jay's talent at sleight of hand and card throwing are extraordinary, but it is also his verbal acuity, his love of language and his ability to construct a narrative for each set-piece that make his performances so distinctive (and so enjoyable).

"What I am after is being able to entertain an audience," Jay told me, "by a combination of my interests in the art form and displaying what skills I have, and how I am able to write these pieces [in a manner] that leaves some mystery."

A tall order and no easy task: sounds like magic to me.

December 3, 2009

LESSONS FROM THE NOT SO DISTANT PAST

History often seems to take place on a stage distant from our own experience—yet the exhibition "Road to Freedom: Photographs of the Civil Rights Movement, 1956-1968," which opened at the Skirball on November 19, reminds us that even our recent past can deliver a strong message for our times.

Road to Freedom is a collection of more than 170 iconic images by more than thirty-five photographers—including Danny Lyon, Morton Broffman, Charles Moore, Bruce Davidson and Gordon Parks—spanning the civil rights movement. It moves from Rosa Parks' arrest in 1955 to Martin Luther King Jr.'s death and funeral in 1968. The show is accompanied by several other exhibitions, including Eric Etheridge's *Breach of Peace.*

Road to Freedom comes to the Skirball from the High Museum of Art in Atlanta, where it was conceived and organized by photo curator Julian Cox. It fits the Skirball's mission to express "the vitality of American democratic ideals," said Skirball associate curator, Erin Clancey: "The images in this exhibition are iconic of the democratic process."

The show is, indeed, striking on several levels. First of all, the historical aspect: Although we may recall the civil rights movement as a series of sit-ins, protests and marches, today, four decades later, it seems like ancient history, a distant memory. It is hard to believe that not so long ago African Americans in this country lived under conditions that claimed to be "separate but equal" but were anything but. A 1962 image by Lyon taken in Georgia shows two water fountains: one, a solid block of metal of the type one sees at schools, beneath the sign: "White." Next to it, a smaller, and in every way lesser, fountain stands under the sign "Colored." It is a simple image that clearly depicts the second-class status once afforded American blacks.

The exhibition takes the viewer on a panoramic tour of the civil rights struggle as it progressed from freedom riders to the early protests in Birmingham to the March on Washington, and the march from Selma to Montgomery. There is also a section on Los Angeles and the 1965 Watts riots (added for the Skirball) as well as one on the funeral of Martin Luther King Jr.

The photographs in this exhibit vividly capture the violence perpetrated against those who dared challenge the status quo: Joseph Postiglione's images of an integrated Greyhound bus set on fire in Alabama; Bill Hudson's of a police dog attacking a young African American man in Birmingham; Charles Moore's photos of fire hoses turned against crowds to disperse and subdue protesters; and a shot of blood-spattered John Lewis and Jim Zwerg, beaten in Montgomery. And there are the photos of the Klan and crosses burning in the night that remain frightening to this day.

This exhibition reminds us that in this battle for human rights and dignity, lives were at stake. A section of the show is devoted to James Chaney, Michael Schwerner and Andrew Goodman, an African American and two white (and Jewish) freedom riders who were arrested by the police and released to Klan members, who murdered them. Another section contains photos from the funeral of King, including Constantine Manos and Bob Adelman's photos of the great civil rights leader lying in his open casket.

The overall effect is immersive and moving.

The role of the press in making the civil rights cause a national one is also a part of this show. Today, when the mainstream media is often derided and facing danger of being dismantled, it is important to recall the outrage, shame and call to action these images produced in everyday citizens, politicians and even in Presidents Kennedy and Johnson.

At the same time, the companion exhibit, Eric Etheridge's *Breach of Peace,* offers a wonderful window into the lives of the 1961 wave of freedom riders, pairing their mug shots with portraits of them today. It is fascinating to read about what motivated them to get involved and what has become of them. Many continued on as political activists, some on the local or even national level—yet, overall, they were just people who became motivated to play a role in history and were, for the most part, changed by the experience. Among those featured are the stories of Bob Filner, then a Cornell student from Queens, today a congressman from San Diego; Jorgia Siegel, then a freshman at Berkeley, today teaching Lamaze classes in Santa Barbara; and Joan Pleune, then a senior at Berkeley, today active in the Granny Peace Brigade protesting the war in Iraq.

As part of the exhibition, one can also watch the award-winning short documentary film, *Voices of Freedom,* which includes both historical footage and present-day interviews with photographers and activists from the era, co-produced by Cox and produced, directed and edited by Neal Broffman, son of photographer Morton Broffman.

Another short documentary, *Partners on the Road to Freedom,* produced with excerpts from the PBS documentary *The Jewish Americans,* on the role of Jewish Americans in the civil rights movement and their common cause with African Americans is shown continuously in the exhibition space. It is definitely worth watching and includes footage of the German-born Rabbi Joachim Prinz's speech at the March on Washington, where he spoke of the Jewish community's bond with the African American community as "solidarity born of our own painful experience."

Two companion exhibitions are also on view. One is *After 1968,* which also was conceived by the High Museum and includes recent and commissioned works by young artists born in or after 1968. The other, titled *An Idea Called Tomorrow,* was co-conceived by the Skirball and the California African American Museum (CAMM) in Exposition Park, and organized by CAMM, showcases works by twelve contemporary artists that address issues of social justice and the active role we all must take in that process. This last show will be on view at both museums.

The combination of the *Road to Freedom, After 1968* and *An Idea Called Tomorrow,* Clancy points out, addresses civil rights' "past, present and future."

After having a few days to let the exhibition's images sink in, I found that I kept thinking of the photographer Moneta Sleet Jr.'s image of a young King reading a book on Gandhi. In all the talk of civil rights and protest, it is easy to forget that the key tactic of King's battle was militant nonviolence. As the exhibition details, protesters were trained to respond to taunts, insults and violence with nonviolence. In the civil rights struggle, practicing nonviolence exposed the weakness of the oppressors, giving protesters the moral high ground and affirming the justice of their cause.

The power of nonviolence is the message that stayed with me long after I finished touring the exhibit—and it is what makes *Road to Freedom* relevant to our times and so fitting for the Skirball, whose own permanent collection highlights the struggle for freedom and the power of democracy.

King was murdered more than forty years ago. He is still celebrated, but his message of nonviolence now seems forgotten.

The conflicts of our recent times, most notably in the Middle East, have been stories of responding to violence with violence in the search for peace and freedom. As the Middle East leaders and their antagonists harden their positions, I wonder what would happen if their own people, along with their supporters at home and throughout the world, were to embrace the militant nonviolence of the civil rights movement.

Given the present situation and current times, it seems an impossible tactic, almost laughable. Yet looking at the photos in the *Road to Freedom*—at what the freedom riders, the protesters and the marchers faced, and the dream they made possible—I wondered whether the true path to peace and freedom wasn't staring me in the face,

December 3, 2009

SILVER JUDAICA STILL SHINES

"How's it going?"

As a tough year ended and a new decade began, it seemed a fair question. While *The New York Times* has looked to bowling alley attendance as a gauge of our nation's condition, I turned to Jonathan Greenstein and his recent auction of silver Jewish ritual art, or Judaica, to determine the health, wealth and current condition of the Jewish community.

On January 11, 2010, J. Greenstein Co., the country's only auction house dedicated to Judaica, held a sale of 185 lots including Kiddush cups, Torah shields, finials as well as rare items as an 1830 Chanukah lamp from Alternberg, Germany, (estimated at $65,000-$85,000), that graced the cover of the auction catalogue.

But first, you may be wondering, who is Jonathan Greenstein and what makes him such an expert?

Born and raised in Brooklyn, NY, Greenstein traces his interest in Judaica to one significant occurrence in his youth: getting kicked out of the Yeshivah of Flatbush in ninth grade.

"My deal with my parents," Greenstein recounted recently, "was that they would let me go to public school if I got a part-time job." So beginning at thirteen and a half, and for the next three and a half years, Greenstein worked part time in an antiques store. The owner, who was not Jewish, allowed the boy to take Judaica items that caught his eye, in lieu of pay. And so, with a twenty dollar Kiddush cup here and an eighty dollar Kiddush cup there, Greenstein began to collect.

Greenstein went on to Brooklyn College, receiving bachelor's and master's degrees in health administration and pursuing a career in home health care. However, he continued collecting and trading Judaica. When he discovered that although there are silver experts, "there is no expertise in Judaica," he took it upon himself to become an expert.

Greenstein is the first to admit that his education is not a formal one; it is all "hands on." What then makes for an expert in silver Judaica?

"Understanding silver, understanding fakes and forgeries, understanding the history of Jewish art, understanding the history of the Jewish people, understanding various art forms," he said, adding that you also need to "understand silver trademarks and similarities between Jewish and non-Jewish art forms of certain periods."

In 2003, Chabad, to which he already was a donor, asked Greenstein to organize a charity benefit featuring an auction of Judaica. The event was a success, and Greenstein's path was set. He got an auctioneer's license in New York and the following year opened up J. Greenstein and Co. He now holds two auctions a year—this month's was his eleventh, and in February he will be begin accepting items for the next, which will take place in June. Greenstein said he no longer collects for himself ("I don't want to compete with my clients"), but he does serve as a consultant to other auction houses and for collectors, advising them on what to buy—and what not to buy; what is fake, for example.

Greenstein believes there are more Judaica fakes than in almost any other field. “You can’t buy Judaica in Israel,” Greenstein says referring to antique Judaica. He warns of fakes in almost every shop on King David and Ben-Yehuda streets in Jerusalem. Most common, he says, are fakes with Russian silver marks—Greenstein recommends anyone making a major purchase ask an independent third party to authenticate. (Greenstein is in the process of writing a textbook to help identify fakes.)

In our conversation, Greenstein waxed poetic about the distinctive characteristics of Ashkenazic work from both Western and Eastern Europe—he described a piece from Poland as magnificent because it expressed “the Jewish soul”; he also admires Sephardic work, with its intricate decorations; and even Judaica from the American Colonial era, such as the work of Paul Revere’s contemporary, Meyer Meyer.

Greenstein still owns a health care company, although he has given up its day-to-day operation. Judaica has taken him places, such as into the homes of major Jewish philanthropists, leaders and celebrities whom he would never have had access to “selling wheelchairs,” he said. That has been one of the most rewarding aspects of his journey, he told me.

He said that the majority of Judaica collectors are fifty and over, often non-observant Jews who respond to the pieces aesthetically or because of a connection between the object’s provenance and the buyer’s own heritage. For some, owning Judaica is a way to express their connection to Judaism. Sometimes the emotional response trumps a rational assessment of authenticity, or, for that matter, value.

Which brings me back to the marketplace. I asked Greenstein how the economic downturn and the Madoff fraud had impacted the current Judaica market.

"A lot more things have become available," he said. "A lot of things popped out of the woodwork in the last couple of years." And the unique pieces did well.

"Quality will always sell," Greenstein explained. "There's a concept of 'fresh' when something hasn't been on the market for twenty or twenty-five years." For example, "there's a menorah that Sotheby's had that had a provenance of 130 years in one family.... It's never been on the market in my lifetime—they estimated [it] at $200,000-$300,000. I went up to $250,000 on behalf of a client—it sold for just under half a million—$470,000 hammer [plus commissions and taxes]. When things are fresh, unseen and sexy, they go for a lot of money."

Which brings us to his January 11 auction. Greenstein offered up 185 lots—of which fifty did not sell or meet their minimum. The top-selling items, with one exception, sold at the low end of the estimate (the Chanukah lamp on the catalogue cover sold for $65,000), and the item that topped the estimate, a silver etrog container, sold for $2,500 above the high estimate. Yet Greenstein assured me that "the sale was our best," selling a total of $550,000 worth of Judaica, a record-breaking sale.

"The Judaica market is very strong," Greenstein said. These days, he said, "people are investing in tangible assets," adding that these "were not 2007 prices." The market, he said, had become rational, not emotional. He added that he is so enthusiastic about the market that he has moved up his next auction from August to June.

So to recap: “How are things?”

Things are not what they were. Quality and “freshness” matters. People who didn’t think they would need to be in the marketplace as sellers, are. As a result, things have rationalized and there is optimism about the future.

Welcome to the new “new.” Welcome to 2010.

January 20, 2010

RETHINKING KASZTNER

"*Killing Kasztner: The Jew Who Dealt With Nazis,*" a new documentary, portrays filmmaker Gaylen Ross' attempt to understand why Reszo (Rudolf) Kasztner, a Hungarian Jewish leader who saved more than 1,600 people in war-time Budapest—more than Oskar Schindler—on the so-called Kasztner train, remains so controversial to this day.

In the course of the film, Ross tells several interrelated stories, including that of Kasztner's rescue efforts during the Holocaust, as well as the stories of his life in Israel, his infamous libel trial (Kasztner was accused of collaborating with the Nazis) and his 1957 assassination by Ze'ev Eckstein, a right-wing Israeli nationalist. Finally the various threads are brought together as Kasztner's daughter meets with her father's murderer and Israel's Yad Vashem acknowledges the importance of Kasztner's rescue efforts, and accepts the Kasztner archive as part of its collection.

Kasztner has been faulted on many counts: for whom he saved and how he chose them (even though Kasztner personally chose very few of the train's passengers, he did put his wife and nineteen of his relatives on the train). For how he saved them—by negotiating with Eichmann and other German officials. And, finally, for not saving more people—600,000 Hungarian Jews were murdered during that time, at one point as many as 12,000 a day—and although Kasztner had received Rudolf Vrba's report on Auschwitz and the Nazi plans for the extermination of Hungarian Jewry, among the accusations made against Kasztner was that he did not sufficiently inform Hungarian Jewry of the report or its contents (a charge he disputed at his Israeli trial).

Kasztner is accused of allowing a few to live so that the others would go to their deaths without protest. As one of Kasztner's daughters asks: "Why Kasztner? Why is Kasztner blamed for everything?"

The emotion Kasztner provokes to this day is striking. It's as if those Jews who survived and those whose relatives were killed have displaced their anger at the Nazis and their own guilt feelings, both for surviving and for not saving others, onto Kasztner.

My father, Bruce Teicholz, knew Kasztner. They met in Budapest shortly after my father's arrival there in early 1942 as a Polish refugee. Kasztner was co-head of the Hungarian Jewish Rescue Committee, my father was co-head of the Polish Jewish Rescue Committee, both of which helped refugees. When the Nazis arrived in Budapest, Joel Brand and Kasztner were the ones to negotiate with Eichmann. My father went underground, leading a group of forgers, couriers, smugglers and fighters who worked with Brand and his wife, Hansi.

My father, who died in 1993, defended Kasztner, believing, as the Supreme Court of Israel would come to conclude, that in impossible circumstances Kasztner did what he could and that lives were saved. “The thing you have to understand about Kasztner,” my father used to say, “is that he was a lawyer.” By which he meant that although Kasztner was never a practicing attorney, his instinct was to negotiate.

One of the arguments made by Merav Michaeli, Kasztner’s granddaughter, in *Killing Kasztner* is that “negotiating” doesn’t fit with how Israelis define their heroes—they prefer fighters or martyrs. Many of Kasztner’s critics argue that it is immoral to have negotiated with the Nazis at all, and that anything gained was done so at an unacceptable price—the lives of Jews.

Kasztner also symbolizes a rift in the Jewish psyche between resistance and accommodation, assimilation and defiance—and in Israel, between Ben-Gurion’s Labor Party and Menachem Begin’s Likud Party. Kasztner worked in a Labor post. The trials sought to bring down the Ben-Gurion government, and Kasztner’s antagonist in his libel trial, attorney Shmuel Tamir, would eventually serve as Begin’s justice minister.

Many in Israel turned against Kasztner when it was revealed at trial that Kasztner gave affidavits in favor of SS officer Kurt Becher, commissar of all German concentration camps and chief of the economic office of the SS in Hungary—which spared Becher from being prosecuted at the Nuremberg War Crimes trials (Becher appeared as a witness). Kasztner also gave affidavits on behalf of Nazis Hermann Krumey and Dieter Wislency, whom he had negotiated with in Budapest. The Israel Supreme Court never reversed the lower court’s judgment about the “criminal and perjurious way” Kasztner saved Becher.

However, the film reveals that Israeli historian Shosanna Barri uncovered documents that indicate that the Jewish

Agency not only knew of Kasztner's dealings with Becher, but that its officials also were in dialogue with Becher themselves, hoping to gain Becher's help in recovering Jewish property and in tracking Eichmann after the war's end. This leaves open the question: Why didn't Kasztner say anything about this? Was Kasztner covering for the Jewish Agency? Was he waiting for them to step forward and clear him? In the end, was Kasztner loyal to a fault?

Finally, Kasztner's assassin, Eckstein, is an extremely compelling character. If you've ever wondered how terrorist organizations recruit assassins or suicide bombers; if you've ever wondered how an educated young person from a good family can be convinced that he needs to take on such a mission—watch this film.

Eckstein explains that his brain was "poisoned" by right-wing extremists who wanted to purge Israel of its corrupt elements, beginning with Kasztner. He says that today he bears no connection to the young man who committed those acts, but he nonetheless accepts full responsibility for his actions. In the film, a meeting between Kasztner's daughter and his assassin is arranged at the daughter's request (the assassin at first refuses, then relents). The meeting, albeit dramatic, is neither cathartic nor revelatory, but does seem to offer Kasztner's daughter a measure of comfort, if not closure.

In light of all this and in spite of all this, the question remains: Why Kasztner? Why was he such a lightning rod?

To understand Kasztner you have to consider the human dimension and consider the man: imagine a person from Cluj, a Transylvanian border city, who arrives in Budapest and appoints himself as the representative of the Jewish people—that takes a certain chutzpah, a certain ego. There is something about Hungarian Jews of that era, in general, and in particular those worldly, assimilated Hungarian Jews who arrived in Budapest as lawyers and journalists (many of whom became playwrights or screenwriters and ended up in Hollywood). They seemed to think of themselves as magicians—charming, entertaining, able to pull a rabbit out of a hat.

Kasztner believed time was on his side—that if Eichmann could be stalled, the war would end.

Was Kasztner arrogant? Was he resented? Was he damned for what he did? And damned for what he couldn't do?

Imagine being a Jew in a room with Eichmann, or riding in an SS staff car with Becher as Jews were being murdered daily; it is as horrifying as it is daunting to contemplate. Lives were in the balance and, thanks to Kasztner, lives were saved—not only those on the Kasztner train, but those that Becher spared in the concentration camps and those my father helped to get false papers or cross the border to safety.

Eichmann and the Third Reich had their own larcenous and murderous ambitions. But did Eichmann and Becher know the war was coming to an end? Did they fear war crimes prosecution? Did Becher give information to the Jewish Agency about "the Becher deposits," confiscated Jewish fortunes in return for Kasztner's affidavit? Nothing happened in a vacuum.

It is a human impulse to second-guess, to judge, to write history as a moral lesson, with right and wrong, winners and losers, heroes and traitors. But history is made by complex characters. We may never know the full truth animating the motives, agendas and politics of Kasztner or his many antagonists. But "Killing Kasztner" makes the case that history is a narrative in flux that can be rewritten as our own understanding of events deepen, and that Reszo Kasztner, in all his complexity, deserves to be remembered.

January 27, 2009

J. D. SALINGER, NOVELIST OF MODERN ANOMIE, DEAD AT 91

J. D. Salinger, the novelist whose *Catcher in the Rye,* was the gateway drug for a generation of teenagers, readers and writers resisting social conformity, and who became almost as famous for being reclusive as he was for his novel and his collections of short stories, died at his home in New Hampshire, at ninety-one. He last published in 1965; Salinger claimed that he continued to write and would no longer be published during his lifetime.

With Salinger's death, the literary world awaits to find out, after more than fifty years of waiting, whether in fact, Salinger left completed work—stories, novels, even poems—and whether it is coherent and intelligible, interesting or out-of-date—whether any of it is good, or even perhaps, great.

In *Catcher in the Rye* he created a teenager character who spoke the feelings of teenagers of all ages, in decrrying the behavior of "phonies." In his subsequent short story collections, *Franny and Zooey* and *Raise High the Roofbeams, Carpenter* Salinger described characters at odds with themselves—and though many readers found them plain odd, they found them compelling. *The Catcher in the Rye* remains one of the perennial best-selling novels, read in schools across the country and the globe, holding a special place on the bookshelves of many. But Salinger's last published stories, increasingly influenced by Salinger's own experiments in eastern thinking, give one pause about what direction his unpublished writing may have taken. Hopefully we will know soon.

After Mark David Chapman murdered John Lennon, he was found with a copy of *The Catcher in the Rye* and various writers and filmmakers have expounded on the connections between the two. John Hinckley, President Reagan's would be assassin also cited the book as a touchstone. Readers formed great attachment to *The Catcher in the Rye* and perhaps this as much as anything was reason for Salinger to remove himself from society and live as a recluse in New Hampshire.

Born Jerome David Salinger in New York City in 1919, his father Sol, worked in the food industry. One of the accounts I read online claims that Salinger's mother was born Marie but called herself Miriam and it was only after his bar-mitzvah that Salinger discovered that she was not in fact Jewish. If true, it may give some foundation for Salinger's lifelong quest for a spiritual identity and his characters own existential dilemmas.

Salinger attended several schools in New York including McBurney before attending Valley Forge Military Academy, and several colleges including New York University and Columbia University's evening program where he attended a writing class taught by Whit Burnett of *Story Magazine* who would publish some of his early work.

In 1941 the *New Yorker* magazine accepted "Slight Rebellion off Madison Avenue," a short story featuring a character named Holden Caulfield.

At that time, Salinger also courted Oona O'Neil, playwright Eugene O'Neil's daughter, who was a teenager at the time—she would eventually marry Charlie Chaplin. The courtship is mentioned in Aram Saroyan's *Trio* his account of the young lives of Oona O'Neil, Gloria Vanderbilt, and Carol Matthau (Saroyan's mother).

It is also reported that around that time Salinger worked on a cruise ship, and perhaps performed on board.

Salinger served in World War Two, landing in France on D-Day and fighting in the Battle of the Bulge. While in France, he met Ernest Hemingway, who impressed Salinger and who was in turn impressed by Salinger's writing—they began a correspondence. Salinger also served in a Counter-Intelligence Unit that interrogated prisoners of war and he was among the first soldiers to enter a recently liberated concentration camp. Shortly thereafter, Salinger reportedly had a nervous breakdown and was hospitalized for combat-related stress in an Army hospital.

Upon his return to the States, Salinger continued to write short stories. "A perfect day for Bananafish" was published in the *New Yorker* and established Salinger as an important contemporary writer. At the same time, Salinger became interested in Buddhism and various variants of eastern religions and religious practices, which he would continue to explore the rest of his life.

With the publication of *The Catcher in the Rye* Salinger who was living in Westport, Connecticutt, moved with his then-wife Claire to Cornish NH, which continued to be his residence until his death. Salinger had two children, Margaret and Matt who survive him.

Salinger continued to publish stories in the *New Yorker,* many of them about the Glass family, until 1965, with "Hapworth 16, 1924," his last published story. After that Salinger claimed that he continued to write but would no longer publish during his lifetime.

At first, Salinger gave interviews to the local paper and high school but he stopped that after a certain while. For awhile, journalists would take it upon themselves to travel to New Hampshire and wait in town for Salinger to pick up his mail and then try and strike up a conversation. Salinger gave his last interview in 1980.

Over the last many decades several persons have written memoirs of knowing Salinger. These include his daughter Margaret, and writer Joyce Maynard who dated Salinger when she was a teenager.

Salinger was protective of his life and his work and over the years sued to block publications biographies, and unauthorized collections of his short stories, or works too closely inspired by his own.

My own Salinger experiences begin with *Catcher In the Rye,* one of four books a bookstore clerk insisted I needed to read, as a teenager, to educate myself (the other three were Aldous Huxley's *Brave New World*, George Orwell's *1984,* and Richard Farina's *Been Down So Long*)—and yes, I became attached to the book. Whenever I had a swimming meet against the McBurney School I thought of Salinger and his description of his fencing team adventure in Catcher—And when we thought of where to meet near Grand Central, we thought of the clock in the Vanderbilt Hotel.

When the *New York Times Magazine* published Joyce Maynard on its cover—I was not alone in developing a crush and felt validated in my attraction when it was reported that she had begun an affair with J. D. Salinger. The fact that Salinger was so much older didn't matter—the creator of Holden was, no doubt, in touch with his inner teenager.

A few years later, I learned that a friend of mine's high school girlfriend had also had a relationship with Salinger which had developed by correspondence. According to the gossip, third hand, Salinger loved to come to New York, much like any tourist, and have tea at the Plaza, see a show and visit friends at the New Yorker and in the city—by being a recluse, he had created anonymity for himself in New York—no one knew what he looked like, no one recognized him.

One summer in the mid-1970s I found myself in the Catalyst bookstore in Santa Cruz. There on the counter by the cash register were two paperbacks, *The Uncollected Stories of J. D. Salinger* volumes 1, and 2. Someone had taken all the stories that Salinger had published over the years in magazines that remained uncollected and published them. I remember holding them in my hands and poring over them, looking at stories I had never heard of. Shortly thereafter, Salinger sued to halt what the publishers called a "samidzat publication" —and those copies were not seen again.

Matt, Salinger's son, is an actor and producer who has lived for many years in LA—I don't know if he still does—I met him once (possibly twice)—he seemed nice and very unaffected. Given that his father wanted at some point to be an actor and/or entertainer—perhaps his father found some pleasure in his son being a working actor who turns up on TV programs with some regularity. In any event, please accept our condolences on your loss.

Although Salinger had one of his early stories optioned for film, the way in which his work was mangled for the screen convinced him to never again allow any of his work to be optioned. Joyce Maynard once commented that Salinger believed that the only one who could ever have played Holden was Salinger himself.

Holden is dead. Long Live Holden.

January 28, 2010

Q & A WITH MEL BROOKS

Mel Brooks is on a hot streak: He was just a Kennedy Center Honoree (along with Dave Brubeck, Robert De Niro, Grace Bumbry and Bruce Springsteen); 20th Century Fox just released *The Mel Brooks Collection* in Blu-ray—a nine-DVD set that includes *Blazing Saddles, Young Frankenstein* and *Spaceballs,* among other classics; and Shout! Factory has released *The 2000 Year Old Man: The Complete History,* a three-CD, one-DVD set that collects the various incarnations in which Carl Reiner, the world's greatest straight man, interviews a visitor who's survived since ancient times and who speaks in a thick Jewish accent to hilarious effect.

Brooks discussed all this, and a bit more, recently in a phone interview from the offices of his production company. I am glad that I taped our conversation, because I was so excited to talk to him that I stopped taking notes after the first few questions. This is an edited version of our conversation.

Tom Teicholz: You were honored recently at the Kennedy Center in Washington, and on TV it looked like you and Bruce Springsteen were kibitzing during the whole show—

Mel Brooks: Oh yeah, well, you know I'm a big fan, and I've got all his—we used to call them records—[and] we were talking about how wonderful the evening was and how honored we felt sitting next to the president.

TT: When the president originally announced your award you sort of interrupted him, too.

MB: I kind of did.... You know, I'm Jewish and irrepressible.

TT: Were you always interrupting people, even as a child?

MB:The minute I could talk, I interrupted people. Because I needed things.

TT: You needed things?

MB: I always needed things. I needed a bagel with cream cheese. I needed things, and I kept asking for them from the minute I could speak.

TT: Carl Reiner, in an interview that's included in *The 2000 Year Old Man* box set, says you were the same way in the room on *Your Show of Shows,* you were the tummler.

MB: Yes, I used to do that in the Borscht Belt in the mountains. I kept the Jewish guests happy around the pool. I amused them with bad jokes, like, 'You can't keep Jews in jail. They eat lox.' Or '[I was dating] a girl who was so thin the waiter said, "Can I check your umbrella?"' Just bad, bad Borscht Belt humor, but, you know, it was a pleasure.

TT: There were a lot of funny guys in that famous writers' room on *Your Show of Shows.* Who, in your opinion, was funniest? Who made you laugh?

MB: They were some of the funniest guys in the world. There was Mel Tolkin, our head writer, [who] had a slight Russian Jewish comedian accent—he was very funny.

TT: I've heard that Mel Tolkin is the underrated comedy genius of that group.

MB: He used to break me up a lot. He was kind of my mentor, too. He helped me, showed me the ropes in comedy writing.

TT: There's also that story about how he recommended a psychiatrist for you.

MB: I went to a psychiatrist, and the guy wouldn't take me. He said, 'I'll find someone else for you, you're too nervous for me.'

TT: Who were some of the other writers who made you laugh?

MB: In the room there were people besides Mel, like Larry Gelbart, very funny and very quick; and Carl Reiner, himself—he used to hang around the writers' room, he was really funny. For a short while, there was Woody Allen. Woody was brilliant: dry wit, you had to listen closely. And then there was Neil Simon, who you never heard. 'Doc' Simon used to whisper in Carl's ear, and Carl would say, 'Neil has the joke,' and then he would say the joke because Neil was too shy to say the joke.

TT: One of the other comments Reiner makes about *The 2000 Year Old Man* that I found fascinating was that after World War II, after the Holocaust, Jewish humor—sounding like an old Jew— was off limits.

MB: Yes, it was not politically correct. It was not in any way correct. We only did the [*2,000-Year-Old-Man* routine] for friends, mostly Jews. So we thought we were on safe ground with the Jewish accent. It was the nature of the questions and answers—Steve Allen said, 'You've got to put it on record.'

TT: It's interesting that a lot of your humor is at the same time outrageous and in some ways old-fashioned.

MB:Yes. Old-fashioned, I always felt, is good. We can go back to Maimonides. Old-fashioned is good. The New Testament, to my mind, is OK, but not quite as hip and brilliant as the Old Testament. So, old-fashioned...is good.

TT: There was a period when your movie work seemed to taper off, before the Broadway version of *The Producers.* Did you think, 'That's it, it's over?'

MB: It's true. When you're first discovered, they make a fuss over you. Four, five movies later, instead of 'It's a Mel Brooks movie!' [you get] 'It's another Mel Brooks movie.' You've got to live with that. But then ten years go by, and it becomes a classic…20th Century Fox is issuing nine Mel Brooks movies with a whole book about my life and pictures from each movie. It's quite good. It's the Blu-ray edition, it's not the hologram edition; you'll have to wait for the hologram edition—that hasn't come out yet. I'm kidding…It's amazing that there's an ebb and flow, and there [are] tides in your life. Suddenly, I'm very hot, with the Kennedy Honors, *The 2000 Year Old Man* and now the Blu-ray edition.

TT: You had this amazing second wind with *The Producers.*

MB: That got the most Tonys ever given to a Broadway show. It's amazing: I just wanted to open the door; I didn't want to break it down.

TT: Seeing the Kennedy Center Honors honoring your work, it turns out you are a song-and-dance man, as much as a comedian.

MB: Turns out that there's a lot of George M. Cohan [in me]. In my neighborhood, we called him Cohen. When I was a kid, we took him as our own. George M. Cohan wrote a lot of Broadway musicals and did what I later followed in his footsteps [doing]. I did the book [for 'The Producers'] together with Tom Meehan. I would write the music and the lyrics.

TT: You could probably put on a revue, 'The Songs of Mel Brooks.'

MB: I probably couldn't. I could get on a stage, get a moderate-sized audience and [sing] songs…Like [breaks into song] :

'Here I am…
I'm Melvin Brooks
I've come to stop the show
Just a ham who's minus looks
But in your hearts I'll grow!
I tell you gags, I'll sing you songs
Happy little snappy tunes that roll along
I'm out of my mind
Won't you be kind?
And, please love
Melvin Brooks.'

That's my first song that I did in the mountains. It would be greeted with a little applause, a little of [he groans], a lot of you'd hear 'English! English!'…because a lot of Jews, when they found out they were in for a night of English, they were very unhappy. I had only a few Yiddish jokes, and my Yiddish to this day is rather limited.

My grandmother spoke Yiddish. Her English wasn't so terrific. She knew a few English words, like 'subway.' She didn't even know fenster for window. She knew 'vindow.' But my mother, who came here when she was three, her name was Brookman, she actually had an Irish accent. You say, 'Why? Why did Mel Brooks' mother have an Irish accent? That's crazy! Why?'

TT: Why?

MB: She was three years old, and when she went to school all the teachers were Irish, and she thought that's the way you speak English. You know [how] we say in the Brooklyn accent 'Thirty-third and Third'? That's all from Ireland.

TT: That's funny.

MB: It's true. I'm half-Irish, without knowing it.

TT: When you originally did *The 2000 Year Old Man,* you were in fact quite young—now you are closer, at least in comedy years, to being 2,000.

MB: That's very funny…[laughs] I'm approaching that 2,000-year-old guy for real!

TT: Does the advice [from] *The 2000 Year Old Man,* still work?

MB: The good jokes still work, even if they are [outdated]. Even if the things are not there anymore. I don't know if the products that I mentioned are still [there].

TT: Nectarines are still a good fruit.

MB: Nectarines are still good.

TT: No fried foods is still good advice.

MB: Yes.

TT: But there are a few better products since then than wax paper.

MB: We mention that! Carl says, 'What about the heart-lung machine?' I said, I believe, on the record: 'That was good. That was good. Hard to get into the medicine cabinet, but that was good.'

Some things are really dated, but we never did anything political. We always did [material about] the human condition. Human behavior. [Carl would say:] 'What were the means of transportation a thousand years ago?' I'd say: 'Fear. A lion would come behind you, you'd move.'

A lot of the jokes from the early record still work. On the first album there are four or five characters…that people don't know about. [The German Psychiatrist, The Third Best Poet, The Astronaut, etc.]

TT: At the Kennedy Center Honors, Carl Reiner said he wanted to get you back in the studio to record again.

MB: We might. But I said to Carl, 'If we do it, let's do it like the first record: Don't tell me what you're going to ask, I don't even want to know the subject. We'll just ad-lib it like we did the first two records.'

TT: Carl Reiner has written several books and several volumes of autobiography. When are you going to write your book, your story?

MB: I'm not old enough yet. I'm only eighty-three. When I get to be ninety-three, I'll start thinking about, 'Maybe I should write an autobiography?'

February 23, 2010

ALSO BY TOM TEICHOLZ

Greetings from Tommywood, (Volume One). Pondwood Press, 2015.

Son of Tommywood, (Volume Two). Pondwood Press, 2015.

Tommywood III: The Column Strikes Back! (Volume Three). Pondwood Press, 2015.

Fast Furious Tommywood (Volume Five). Pondwood Press, 2015.

Close Encounters of the Tommywood Kind (Volume Six). Pondwood Press, 2015.

Wilshire Boulevard Temple and the Warner Murals: Celebrating 150 Years by Tom Teicholz, Oro Editions, San Francisco, CA 2014.

The Jewish Role in American Life, Casden Insitute Annual Study, Volume 1, by Barry Glassner, Hillary Lachner, and Tom Teicholz, USC / Casden Institute, Los Angeles, CA, 2008.

Like No Other Store: Bloomingdale's and the Revolution in American Marketing by Marvin Traub and Tom Teicholz, Times Books/Random House, New York, New York, 1993.

The Trial of Ivan The Terrible: State of Israel vs. John Demjanjuk by Tom Teicholz, St.Martin's Press, New York, New York, 1990.

Conversations with Jerzy Kosinski, edited and with an introduction by Tom Teicholz, University Press of Mississippi, Jackson, Mississippi, 1993.

Conversations with S. J. Perelman, edited and with an introduction by Tom Teicholz, University Press of Mississippi, Jackson, Mississippi, 1995.

Other books and anthologies containing Tom Teicholz's work:

Encyclopedia Judaica, Second Edition. Tom Teicholz, American Film and TV editor., 2006.

Conversations with Isaac Bashevis Singer, University Press of Mississippi, Jackson, Mississippi, 1992.

Writers at Work, Volume 8, The Paris Review Interviews, Viking/Penguin, New York, 1988.

ACKNOWLEDGEMENTS

I am grateful to The Jewish Journal where this work originally appeared in print; and to the editors, proofreaders, and designers who made my work more readable; and to The Huffington Post for allowing me to repost my work there.

I also want to thank the contributors to The TOMMYWOOD Collection IndieGogo campaign for their support and generosity which made publication possible, most notably my tzadiks, hoochems and benefactors: Sandy Climan, Bracken Darrell, Lawrence Schoen, Toni and John Schulman, Bob & Cori Davenport, Peter Graham and Heidi Drymer, Ken & Teri Hertz, Wally & Helen Weiss, Dede Arnholz, Chuck Leavitt, Sharon Nazarian, Chris Pilkington, Stacy and Massimo Pinello, Robert & Edie Parker, Annie Scichili, and Richard Wolloch.

There is more to a book than just writing its content. You need talented people to successfully prepare it for publication. The reason this book looks so terrific is because of designer Devin Tanchum and the very talented folks at Rare Bird Lit, notably my book guru Tyson Cornell and his excellent associates Alice Elmer and Violet Sarosi, as well as Winona Leon (who did the design work for my IndieGogo Campaign). I also want to thank John Vaskis and John Trigonis at IndieGogo for teaching me so much about crowdfunding and helping make this book possible.

ABOUT THE AUTHOR

Tom Teicholz is an award-winning journalist, producer, and content consultant who has created print, video, and social media content for Intel, Logitech, The Museum of Tolerance, and The Milken Family Foundation as well as for several not-for-profits and private clients. His work has appeared in *The New York Times* Sunday magazine, *The Los Angeles Review of Books*, *The Los Angeles Times* Op-Ed page, Newsweek.com, *The Paris Review, The New Yorker's 'Talk of the Town', Narrative Magazine*, Forbes.com and the *Huffington Post.* He lives with his wife and daughter in Santa Monica, CA.

www.ingramcontent.com/pod-product-compliance
Lightning Source LLC
Chambersburg PA
CBHW020626110726
47899CB00002B/670

* 9 7 8 0 9 8 8 3 9 6 4 7 0 *